THE WAY YOU MAKE ME FEEL

20 LESSONS IN CUSTOMER SERVICE

DONNOVAN SIMON

iUniverse, Inc.
Bloomington

The Way You Make Me Feel
20 Lessons in Customer Service

iUniverse books may be ordered through booksellers or by contacting:

iUniverse
1663 Liberty Drive
Bloomington, IN 47403
www.iuniverse.com
1-800-Authors (1-800-288-4677)

Because of the dynamic nature of the Internet, any web addresses or links contained in this book may have changed since publication and may no longer be valid. The views expressed in this work are solely those of the author and do not necessarily reflect the views of the publisher, and the publisher hereby disclaims any responsibility for them.

ISBN: 978-1-4620-0253-5 (sc)
ISBN: 978-1-4620-0254-2 (ebook)

Printed in the United States of America

iUniverse rev. date: 03/28/2011

Contents

Acknowledgements

So many persons have been influential in assisting me in getting this book to print. Some of them may not have considered their role to be as significant as I did. Firstly, I want to say a heartfelt thanks to Janet Sue Rush for initiating a conversation which served as the embryo of the idea for this work. Who would have known that an ice-breaking conversation would have triggered such desire? Her willingness to contribute even further by writing the foreword doubles my appreciation. She has, in her illustrious professional career, influenced many professionals. I have been fortunate to get a double dose of benefit from her experience.

My colleagues at SMART, Vin Seunath, Heather Eeles and Becky Saunders contributed validation for the idea and endorsement for the overall effort. Additionally, Becky spent many hours reviewing the chapters and providing welcome feedback on context and structure from a reader's perspective. No work, however simple, could be produced without additional eyes and minds which provide guidance and reality.

Danielle and Jordin, my kids, were deprived of many hours of their parent time as I tried to channel my ideas into the limited hours available for writing. While they may still be too young to understand, I know I diverted many hours of attention that they should have had, into getting this work done. If Danielle and Jordin did not understand; my wife, Hermalyn, did. She did not object to the separation as I focussed on getting this work to press. She took time to read, and comment, while providing moral support along the way. That level of support was invaluable and deeply appreciated. She believed in me and what I wanted to achieve, which counts even more.

There are many others who helped, even with simple words of encouragement or queries on when the book would be available for purchase. I am grateful to everyone and dedicate this work to all who appreciate the value of the customer and the power of positive feelings. Hopefully this work inspires action in others. If it does, all the trade-offs would be worth it.

Donnovan D. Simon

Foreword

Customer Service........the competitive edge in any business today is all about how we make our customers feel. At a time when executives are concerned about being the "right size," or having the "right technology," or becoming the "low cost producer". Donnovan Simon reminds us in his book *The Way You Make Me Feel* that companies overlook their most important competitive weapon-their customers. A company whose customers are happy with its products and services is virtually unbeatable. It can command a higher price, its customers are more loyal and it has more time to adapt to changes in market conditions, technology or labour costs. Customer Service is all about "the experience" and the interaction between people. Indeed it is about the "way you feel" after your customer service encounter. Simply stated "Sales is Service and Service is Sales" demonstrates a company's business strategy in focusing on the customer experience. After reading *The Way You Make Me Feel* you will definitely ask yourself the question........are you on the leading edge or bleeding edge of customer service?

At last a book that convincingly demonstrates through examples that satisfying the customer is the key to long-run company profitability. Practicing the obvious still makes sense into today's business environment. Donnovan shares with his readers real life customer service experiences and advises them with strategic "prescription" remedies for improvement. His approach is simple and to the point so at the end of the day there is only one question you need to ask…."how did you make your customers feel?"

To serve means putting someone besides you first. The golden rule in service is *"make me feel important about myself."* The "Customer is King" resonates throughout all levels of any successful organization for it is this attitude that establishes customer loyalty and brand retention. You will want to read the 20 Prescriptions offered in *The Way You Make Me Feel* on how your organization can capitalize on world class opportunities that will better serve your customers. *The Way You Make Me Feel* will inspire and motivate you to take a second look at your own customer service. Thank you Donnovan for making me feel terrific about my customers.

Janet Sue Rush
President
The Rush Company
www.janetrush.com

Introduction

Probably the most important management fundamental that is being ignored today is staying close to the customer to satisfy his needs and anticipate his wants. In too many companies, the customer has become a bloody nuisance whose unpredictable behaviour damages carefully made strategic plans, whose activities mess up computer operations, and who stubbornly insists that purchased products should work.

Lew Young, Editor-in-Chief, Business Week [1]

In the early part of spring I was invited to a session attractively titled "Sales is Service and Service is Sales" by one of our vendors. Catchy line. Unlike many other times when I was invited to some canned sales presentation disguised as an attempt to enlighten and educate, I opted to attend this one. I even passed the invitation to other managers and encouraged them to attend as well. I had limited expectations of the entire affair. When I arrived at the location, there were very few people there and my already low expectations seemed reasonable. I did not know of the presenter prior to the invitation and the Google search did not translate into excitement. In my mind, other invitees had the same view and therefore opted to use their time more productively, hence the low attendance. I learnt later that we were the only ones invited.

The next three hours were special. It inspired this work among other initiatives that I have triggered within teams that I managed. The presenter was an old school performance consultant who forced me, and the entire audience, to focus on some very basic components of customer service. Who would have thought that an event which was geared to sell me on the virtues of a new piece of software would have led to a whole new approach to delivering service to customers? Not that the issues raised were by any means revolutionary; they weren't. What happened was the application of a new perspective to what I had spent the better part of fifteen years doing every day.

For my entire career I had the pleasure of providing service to customers. However, despite all the excellent training, coaching and other development activities that I had been involved in, it had never dawned on me how very basic an approach should be to providing customer service. Not that the training, coaching and other development activities were a waste. Unnecessary complexity was always added to the perspectives, which resulted in the approaches being more challenging than they really should have been. It all made sense but sometimes seemed really hard to do. Now, here I was, finally realizing that customer service was about how we made the other person feel when they interacted with us. Nothing more; nothing less. In the middle of all of this were processes, tools, systems and a range of other things. Every service interaction is measured by the way we made the customer feel. The application of the processes, tools and systems, are contributors and do not alter the fact that how the customer feels in the end is paramount.

This book is a collection of my experiences as a customer and how each made me feel. Having first-hand reactions has allowed me the opportunity to prescribe solutions which would have generated different feelings which, in turn, may have changed the outcome of the interaction. In some cases the results may not have changed. Necessity dictated that. Within the prescriptions are some fundamentals that every customer service professional should take into consideration and apply as often as possible. Each interaction with a customer is a contribution to an overall perception that each customer develops of that organization. Additionally, the grand total of the emotions triggered by these interactions ultimately determine whether that organization remains viable, profitable and relevant.

In an era of fierce competition and uncertain times, it is increasingly important that all persons charged with directing the affairs of an organization ensure that all teams involved in interacting with customers understand the power of the way people are made to feel, and how this translates into the survival, success and possible extinction of the organization. In a recent edition of *En Route*, the on-board magazine for Air Canada, an article from the President and CEO of Air Canada, Calin Rovinescu captured my attention. It was titled, *Putting Customers First*. He said

"Over the last couple of years, we have invested heavily in new aircraft, in expanding our network and other initiatives to make travel easier. Still, we know customer loyalty depends upon one simple thing: the way we interact with our customers."

This was very refreshing to see as, for many years, Air Canada had taken severe criticism for its customer service. With competition from new players, global market conditions and the volatility in the price of oil, Air Canada struggled to achieve profitability. That the organization accepted the importance of focussing on the customers' needs is a step in the right direction. As the article summarized, *"We are determined to have customer service embedded in the Air Canada DNA".* This resonated with me, not only because of the simplicity of the approach, but also because it validated my view that organizational recovery is a combination of strategies which must include a focus on how customers feel.

The tenets reflected in each prescription in this book are by no means exhaustive of all the ideas on how to build a world class customer service organization. They do however reflect options that are likely to be useful in more situations than not. They also reflect themes that all organizations should include in the formulae that they develop to achieve and maintain their success. The efforts made to develop successful models are easily condemned to being normal if they are not supported by effective implementation and passionate reinforcement. Humans are subject to error and those managing support organizations are challenged to have their team members develop and maintain habits that consistently result in extraordinary customer experiences. Each customer, no matter what the circumstance, goes into each interaction with a customer service organization with the desire to leave satisfied. Satisfied does not mean always achieving all they wanted, it means having a feeling which reflects an acceptance of the outcome and pleasure with the treatment. *The Way You Make Me Feel* is geared towards refreshing professionals on the need to ensure that the fundamentals of human interaction are instilled in their operations. It is a reflection of reality and the need for reality. Overall, it is an expression of a customer who has a simple objective, which is to feel important and be treated with respect.

Chapter 1 – Reading the rules

It is a steamy day in July 2010 and I am in Kingston, Jamaica at the National Library of Jamaica which is a part of the Institute of Jamaica. As a high school student back in the early to mid 1980s, I had spent many hours in this building researching a range of subjects, primarily to meet the requirements for my General Certificate in Education (GCE) Advanced level History course. These courses required lots of deep diving into journals which were not standard offerings in the public library. Here I was, two decades later, on another quest for information contained in old books and periodicals. My experience starts at the registration table where I am asked to fill out a registration form in order to access the library's material. No problem. Having done all that was required I advised the clerk that I needed to search through some material on microfilm which was on the second floor of the building.

Twenty years could be considered a long time, however, not much had changed in the research room. Old brown furniture, old microfilm readers and the same manual processes remained. There were a number of notices, in small print, all around. They may have been important but who makes an effort to read fine print? Not me. I explained my goal to the clerk; advising that I would need as much help as possible. I was researching old newspapers for a period of over a century which would require, not only viewing the material, but also verifying the accuracy of some data that I had already collected. What was great was that the clerk understood that I would need help in order to be successful, which, like most persons doing research, was a standard occurrence. Not only did she display that understanding, which would have likely come from being in the role for several years and encountering many clients like myself, she took the time to ensure that all the users understood how to use the microfilm readers. My feelings were positive based on the service that was being provided. I was excited about the project as it was likely to lead to the publication of my first book. She did not know that. All that excitement was compounded by a warm feeling that came from the recollection of my school years. I felt really great that morning.

The hours spent in the library that day were productive and ignited my desire to go back to complete, or attempt to, the research. I needed to print some of the items that I had viewed. This required paying prior to collecting the printouts. That should be easy I thought. I walked down the flight of stairs to the cashier who offered a blank stare as she stretched for the papers that I had to give to her. She appeared to be in some discomfort and seemed woefully disinterested in the fact that I was there, worse yet, she appeared inclined to finish whatever she had been doing prior to attending to me. The next few seconds were priceless. A pained look followed by a strained smile, preceded her saying in a low voice, "Oh, I am having cramps". I commiserated quickly hoping my discomfort would not have been very obvious. Never in my over four decades had I, or would have thought that, one would have experienced that revelation from a customer service professional. Not that I did not care about the pain she may have been feeling but what did that have to do with how she eventually made me feel?

Within five minutes of being served by her, I felt unimportant, uncomfortable and uncaring. None of these feelings were what I had expected when I went to this cashier. I merely wanted to pay my bill. I left, firstly wishing she would feel better quickly and then hoping I would not see her again lest I had the same experience. The transaction was done with the least interactivity possible and I concluded that she really did not care how that experience would have made me feel, after all, I needed her more than she needed me.

My next visit was a few days later. With the same bounce in my steps as I had on the previous visit, I entered the library only to be checked by the warden who advised that the large envelope which I had with all my papers had to be left with him. Yes, the empty envelope. Of course, on my last visit I was allowed to take it with me. Maybe in the eyes of the person on duty then, I did not pose a risk which clearly I did this time around. I was a little peeved at the conclusion drawn by the gentleman and for a moment thought of leaving instead of complying. The greater purpose of my visit led to the decision to leave my empty envelope with him and proceed to the reading room. After all, the guy was only following the rules and therefore he was right. He surely did not care that I was a forty something professional who was not likely to behave the same way fifteen year old high school students did. The fact that he made me feel that way would likely not be something he was concerned with either; he was there to limit the theft of material from the research rooms.

Once in the research room, I proceeded to complete my request forms as I had done on my previous visit. A young man nicely dressed in a pink shirt and matching tie, took my requests and started to search for the items I wanted. I was likely to have each item for only a few minutes; not that anyone would know or likely care. I completed and submitted the forms in batches until he stated in a "matter of fact" tone that I was allowed only five requests for the day and he would therefore not accept any more. He pointed me to the rule, in fine print, on a notice board. He emphasised that I had already gone over my quota for the day. For a moment I was speechless, the queried the basis on which the quota was set. He defensively explained that he was not aware of why it was set, while restating the rule.

At the time this was happening, I was one of only two users of the facility. Being advised that there was a rule which limited how many items I could have requested, unless I advised them prior to getting there seemed ridiculous, to say the least. What was even more shocking was the lack of logic or explanation that the young man provided. Although I was fuming at the way he had communicated and handled my query about "the rule", I left the desk and continued my research. While I was in no position to determine whether the rule was practical, reasonable and built on great merit or not, I knew the room was not busy and that my requests would have consumed no more time had I requested a smaller number of items. In the opinion of whoever made the rule, I, the customer, should apply a generic limit on the amount of work I could do without prior notification, no matter what the circumstances. As a customer, I felt angered by the presumption and also the "abiding by the rules" approach that the young man applied.

I took the items that he provided and resigned myself to doing as much as I could. It would have required several visits with "prior notice" in order for me to achieve what I wanted to do; I did not have that much time. Already I was devising ways to get the information required. I needed to complete my project, which was already way overdue. I was prepared to suffer the negative emotions in order to get my work done. It was one of those cases where there was no option which would have taken me to my desired outcome. Like others who had experienced the "reading of the rules" of the organization, I was a victim of the source of my requirements.

About an hour later after scouring through many pages of microfilm, I went back to the desk to collect the last of my requests. The thought of having to relate to the young man did not sit well with me. I had gotten into the "I want to speak to your manager" mentality which on second thought would have achieved little if anything. Usually in organizations like these, speaking to the manager never helps. About an hour later, I noticed that the young man who had advised me of the rules was relieved by the young lady who had served me on my previous visit. I approached the desk with a question and she quickly recognized me from our previous encounter and proceeded to assist me. Having answered my question, I explained the need for several other items which would take me over my quota for the day. There was no push back. She had an appreciation of what I was trying to do and agreed to assist. I am sure she knew the rules however she made an effort to meet my needs as much as she could reasonably do. I made no special request or asked for any special favours. In fact, in my view, my submissions were basic and should have been seen that way.

I appreciated the pleasant, professional approach she demonstrated and while she did not know it, she evoked a positive emotion which quickly replaced the seething that started with my encounter with the young man. A few hours passed during which she helped me with several other requests. Before leaving, I asked her name and advised that I would ensure that the organization's management was made aware of the stellar job she had done which exceeded my expectations. In a humble voice she reluctantly gave me her name, Ms. Worrell. She explained that it was her job to provide excellent service and in her view, she had done nothing special. She had.

I left the National Library of Jamaica thinking of the various experiences I had as their customer. Three of the service providers did not care much about how I may have felt as a customer of their organization. It may have been that they were not trained to think like that. One person however did which made the question of training void. The same factors which drove Ms. Worrell to provide service far exceeding any of the other service providers could have influenced the other behaviours, but they did not. I was also prepared to wager that those that made me feel bad had behaved that way before, and would do it again. In the same breath, I was confident the Ms. Worrell would offer exemplary service to other users of the library.

Organizations need rules and standards to ensure that repeatable processes exist to drive acceptable levels of efficiency. The designers of these rules, however well-intentioned, are usually not those executing the rules. This limits their ability to evaluate the impact of the execution on the customer experience. Often therefore, customers and service providers get bland experiences which paint the organization as insensitive to customers' feelings. It is critical when the execution plans are being developed that the practitioners are taught the importance of acting in a manner which respects the feelings of the customers involved in these interactions. The inclusion of gestures, statements and other actions which reflect humanity are critical to being successful in customer service. No customer wants to have negative emotions triggered, especially in situations where they have a clear choice of providers. Options don't always exist. My experience at the National Library was an example of one of those situations where there was no alternative. In those situations the negative feelings are compounded by the dilution of one's options. Where there is no purchasing power the pain of the experience is amplified.

The National Library may have had good reasons for the rules. It may have worked effectively in the past and delivered the outcomes that the management desired. In my case, they clearly did not, and, but for the discretion of Ms. Worrell, I could easily have failed to achieve my objective. It could be argued that the male clerk was the anomaly in the equation and in fact, it worked the way it was expected to. Could the same be said of the cashier and the warden at the door? It is unlikely that 75% compliance could be considered acceptable which suggests that there is an opportunity for more work at this organization to achieve the customer experiences which they hope for. More customers are likely to feel the same way I did, or worse, if it is not addressed quickly.

Prescription

- **Explain the organizational principles to all employees**

Many organizations implement customer service models aimed at achieving consistency and efficiency only. Within these models, the representatives executing the requirements are likely to become robotic based on the structure that has been established. If there is no training provided on how to effectively utilize judgement, you achieve output which is "correct" but not one that meets or exceeds the expectations of a customer. The challenge of every manager with this dilemma would be to determine what was most important. I would suggest that the customer be considered most important in the equation.

My recommendation to this organization would be to develop a program which provides employees with training in the application of judgement. Not only is it important to teach them about judgement but also the effective ways to apply that skill in order to meet both the organizational and customer expectations. Additionally, I would recommend that as part of the program the rules be removed and replaced by periodic personal objectives. This would allow the employees greater freedom to apply judgement as required to achieve these objectives.

I would be willing to wager a small amount that this team has never been provided with any training on organizational culture. The image that the organization wants to maintain is not a core part of how the employees operated. All organizations should ensure that time is taken to convey the principles of the organization before employees begin the tasks in their roles. In the process they would also learn how these principles are to be communicated to everyone outside the organization. It should be a fundamental part of any organization and will add value, and perspective, to the things employees do. It will also serve as the point of reference when there is need to coach an employee, especially those who serve as the face of the organization.

Note: On a visit to the National Library about six months later, I noticed that Ms. Worrell had been recognized by the organization as the "Customer Service Representative of the Year". That was well deserved.

Chapter 2 – Could this be a sale?

It was time for our family to look at getting a new vehicle, not because the two cars we had were in bad shape, but a vehicle seating four persons no longer worked for us. Our kids were getting to the stage where more leg room was required. I had delayed actively searching for a while to ensure that the financing of the purchase did not create any undue financial challenge. It was now the time and I wanted to do it quickly.

I had done my research on the vehicles that I wanted to explore. There were three options. Practicality was one of the biggest factors on my decision matrix. Fuel efficiency, cost, safety and resale value were a few others that I knew would factor in the ultimate decision. I made a call to a local Honda dealer and advised the very pleasant person at the other end of my interest. Within a few minutes I was connected with a sales rep that quickly made an appointment for me to meet with him the next day. Within an hour, I got a call from the sales manager of the organization who advised me that he was aware of my appointment the next day and that he wanted me to contact him if there was anything that would make it easier for me to arrive at the decision to get the vehicle that best met my needs. All went well on my visit, including the test drive. I was impressed with the effort taken to understand my need and advise me on what would likely be the best purchase options. What stood out most was the effort the sales rep made, without trying to be "cheesy". He offered a promotional discount without being asked and overall tried to give me a good deal.

Not being one to make purchases without a comparative analysis, I drove to a nearby Hyundai dealer to look at a similar vehicle. The criteria that would determine the ultimate selection remained the same and I was open to their offer once it met my needs. I opted to visit this dealership because we had bought there before. That purchase was a pleasant experience and I thought it would make sense to go there again. On entering the sales department, there were three people who appeared to be employees. I was greeted with a hello by the lady at the desk which I returned. This was followed by silence and a questioning look from her. I knew from her look that she wanted me to state the purpose of my visit, however I delayed to allow her the chance to actually ask me. Instead, she said hello again to which I promptly responded with another hello. Stalemate. There was a young man standing there who figured he needed to break the ice and forcefully asked if there was any way that he could assist me. His tone was almost scary and in my opinion, it was more aimed at quickly ending the stalemate rather than a genuine invitation to help. I advised him of the vehicle I wanted to look at and he summoned another employee to address my need. The employee quickly came over and asked what I wanted to know. I will admit that I was a little taken aback by the approach of the sales rep as he asked what I wanted to know and exploded with information on all the wonderful features of the vehicle. I asked a few questions based on the information he was providing and he made sure to advise me that it was a luxury vehicle and to that extent those features were standard. His tone suggested that

I should have known that. Clearly, in his view, I knew little about luxury vehicles even though I wanted to see one.

I started feeling anxious, however I continued with my exploration and requested a test drive. After providing my driver's licence, as was the practice at all the other places I had visited, we were off for the drive. After a few instructions, a cloud of silence descended on us. The discomfort that came with the silence made the cloud even heavier. After a few minutes he asked that I make a turn which effectively would take us back to the dealership. Like him, I wanted to get back too. I was relishing the painful environment no more than he was, although I was hoping that he was in more pain than I was. In my mind, a sales person who opted not to effectively engage a customer, for whatever reason, deserved to have a painful experience. So, I did just that. After a bit of driving around, I went back to the dealership where he asked me if there were any other questions. I was about to walk to my car when he extended his hand for a handshake and asked my name. I gave him my first name and left. Clearly, at least to me, I was not considered a prospect. That was a fair conclusion as he had no contact information, neither was he aware of anything else which would help him determine my likelihood to purchase.

I drove home wondering how I would have felt had I been the owner of that business watching or listening to that episode. There could have been no sane businessman who would not have been appalled at the service provided. I figured it would be useful to talk to the sales manager of the business about my experience. Like many other customers, I was not looking for recourse, but figured feedback would help them make it better and stay in business. I called, spoke to the sales manager, and concluded that the behaviour of Jared, the sales person, reflected the way the business was managed. I told the sales manager the way things went, and how I felt. His only response, having said that I would not be making a purchase there was "is there anything I could do to change your mind?" He too did not know my name or what my needs were and I ended the conversation with him, as I had ended the interaction with the sales person, knowing that there was nothing he, or anyone there, could do to get my business.

The next day I called the Honda sales person, Norman, to see if I could come by to see the vehicle again. This time I took my wife to have her contribute to the decision. He was very accommodating and facilitated a test drive for her. What was interesting was the effort he made to determine what she wanted to see and know about the vehicle, without losing sight of my initial expectations. He also made a deliberate effort to discuss needs, and wants, before getting into trying to make a deal. I had called before to make some proposals on the final price, which he acknowledged but did not make it the primary focus of our meeting. Finally we went back to his office and he made a counter proposal which was not as pleasing as I would have wanted. By then, I was sold on the service and would not have haggled to gain a few hundred dollars. He actually seemed surprised when I agreed to his offer. The deal was done. I had decided to pay cash which eliminated the paperwork that he would otherwise have had to do. It was the perfect situation for him. It was driven in many ways by the way he made me feel throughout the entire experience. The process thereafter went smoothly and the next afternoon I was able to collect my new car.

I arrived at the agreed time to collect my new vehicle. I

was excited as it was my first SUV purchase. How smoothly the experience had gone to that point added to the pleasure. On arrival, I was taken on a final check of the vehicle to ensure I was pleased with its condition. I was also given a quick lesson on the key features of the vehicle and how to operate them. Additionally, the attendant took time to check all the other things like the lug tool, spare tires and storage compartments before handing it over to me. This was the icing on the experience as not only was he really professional, he allowed me the chance to ask questions. He was in no hurry. You could argue that the sale was already done and therefore he did not need to care as much as he did, however, it was clearly a habit of how they made people feel at the organization and I concluded that it translated to all customers, including myself.

Neither Norman nor any of the other persons involved with getting me the new vehicle would have known how I felt about the entire process, or the comparative experience that had influenced my decision. They did not need to ask me how I felt or explain that they were trying to sell me a car. By the actions and attitudes that were displayed, I knew they cared about how my experience went and they took the right steps to ensure that only positive emotions were triggered throughout the process. If in the end the vehicle did not perform the way I expected, there would be a greater level of tolerance, and confidence in the company, based on the experience I had in the acquisition process.

From the experience, I kept wondering whether or not people in roles to deal with customers always made the connection between what they did and the success and profitability of the business they own or work for. If they did, there would always therefore be an effort to convert customer interest into revenue. What other ultimate goal could there be? Clearly, all the dealerships that I visited operated with simple goals – sell vehicles. Each employee would have been placed in roles which facilitated that ultimate goal. In the case of the Hyundai dealership, the employees did not seem to think it necessary to present that to me. They may have done it for other customers otherwise they would have been out of business before. What they missed, in my view, was the opportunity to do it all the time. Why would they not? Is there an acceptable limit to success? What about the possibility that this could be a repeat customer or one who refers friends to organizations that provide great service? The employees of the Honda dealership received limited competitive challenge in this process. They won too easily. This slam dunk opportunity to score a sale, as provided by the Hyundai dealer, was not good business but it happens every day.

Prescription

- **Outline the impact of everyone's goal to organizational success**

The degree to which employees can correlate their role to the purpose of the organization will impact the behaviours they develop within their roles. If this is discussed, and effectively reinforced, an organization can obtain employee performance which leads to organizational success. On the contrary, failure to effectively get this correlation leads to organizational under-performance and in some cases, closure. It is therefore important that while orienting employees on the organization culture and performance expectations, that an effort be made to establish the organization's success equation and how the employee contributes to it. In the case of these companies, I suspect that the sales persons were oriented differently. One was clearly aligned to what led to success for the organization while the other was not. What may have caused this?

Business owners enter into the challenging world of business with the intention of having a positive return on investment. Market forces and other factors may contribute to the demise of many businesses. When things happen outside the control of a business owner, which leads to business failure, they can at least feel content that they did all things possible to achieve business success. It is therefore important that owners convey their goal to employees throughout the organization. The management of the organization should also be cognizant of this and operate in a manner to ensure that this is realized. If they don't, they should be quickly replaced as lost business is not easy to recover. I would suggest that the sales manager at the Hyundai dealership be replaced. Why? I don't think he is instilling the right habits in his team. Where operational alignment is missing, it is unlikely that overall organizational goals will be met. Clearly this Hyundai business is losing money through missed sales, which may not be accounted for, as interactions like mine are not recorded. How many similar events occur every month? Who knows?

Chapter 3 – Is it all about cost?

Have you ever been in a situation where someone providing service thinks the cost of the product or service is most important to you? How did it make you feel? I was in Ottawa, Ontario a few years ago on a business trip. After a long day of meetings, I wanted to relax and have a nice dinner before retiring for the day. I was travelling with a colleague who suggested we visit a Milestones restaurant that was close to the hotel where we stayed. I acted on his suggestion. Although I had been there a few times, I did not know much of the restaurants in the area. We had invited two colleagues from the local branch to join us; it was a nice spring evening so we opted to enjoy the patio as suggested by the host. Our server, Ashley, soon arrived, greeted us warmly and started her service with an offer for drinks. Ashley was gorgeous and had a very amiable demeanour. As is typical when a gorgeous server has to interact with four gawking men, the flirting started early and while Ashley was a great sport, on a few occasions it was clear that we were testing her patience a little more than she may have wanted. She did not lose her composure even for a moment and for the two and a half hours that we spent there; she was professional, entertaining and keen to meet our needs. At all stages of the evening her main focus was making sure we had a good time. Between drinks, appetizers and the main course, she was the ultimate host.

After a wonderful evening of good food, good company

and excellent service, we ensured that Ashley was adequately tipped in recognition of the service that she provided. It was my hope that she recognized our appreciation. Being someone who travelled around for a little bit, I was always conscious of the need to tip generously for great service. Not only did it reward the provider, but it set the stage for them to continue providing the same excellent service. In my mind, tipping well made it easier for her to make the next customer feel good as well.

With the images of Ashley, as well as the wonderful experience in my mind, the next evening was a struggle to decide whether we went back to Milestones or try another restaurant in the area. We opted for variety; after all, getting different experiences would provide some local knowledge for the next time we were in the area. After a few wrong turns, we got to the mall where there was a collection of restaurants. We chose a restaurant named Scores, as my colleague and I thought it would have been a southern style offering which was different from our previous night's experience. While not overly famished, we wanted to have a solid meal. The name of the restaurant implied it was not a fast-food joint. The hostess quickly found us a table and advised that a server would be with us shortly. Shortly was not as short as we had expected. While the delay was noticeable, we were not bothered. We took the time to have a chat about the location and the likely service we would get based on the time it was taking for them to find a server for our table. We laughed at the thought that maybe they thought we were big eaters and did not want to serve us. After about fifteen minutes, which felt like an hour, a server came to our table and in a very nonchalant way asked what we were interested in having. Even before we answered she whipped to a page in the menu where the value meals were and advised us of the special low-priced buffet items available. For a moment I wondered why she would do that. She did not take the time to get an answer from us. She did not know what we were interested in eating. Maybe our appearance suggested that we needed value meals. If that were the case, so did everyone in the restaurant.

My colleague made his selection quickly and I followed suit. There were limited choices on the menu which we had more than enough time to review prior to her arrival. She left us without an offer for drinks. I figured we were in for one of those memorable poor service events and tried to relax and watch it unfold further. I cannot recall the servers name; chances are she did not say and never had a name tag. I do remember her countenance and it was by no means one that encouraged us to be mischievous. Part of my colleagues order included a selection of soup served on the buffet line. He went to get his soup however the selection he would have preferred was not available and the person manning the station could not say if it would have been replenished; so he settled for the second option. He did think it was delicious. Good.

It took another twenty minutes before our meals were served. Not that they were anything gourmet but I concluded that they were short on staff which led to the rather slow service. Having provided us with our meals, our server left. I sped through mine and made a wager that we would not see her again until we wanted our bill. I was correct. We ate without a query and upon completion she appeared and asked if were interested in coffee or dessert. Of course, neither my colleague nor I accepted the offer. In fact, I had already planned to go back to Milestones to get the banana cheesecake delight that I had the night before. I paid the bill and did not add a tip. At the time I was somewhat rebuffed by the nonchalance and lack of focus on making us feel special. While there was no behaviour that could have been considered rude or unprofessional, I felt like the only goal they had was getting me something to eat with as little interaction, or pleasantries, as possible. It seemed all mechanical. Maybe having smiling, playful customers took away from the efficiency of the staff. As we drove back to our hotel, we wondered if it was a matter of her having a "bad day". Even with that thought, we could not help but wonder if it was the standard behaviour for the servers in that restaurant. If it was the standard, they were setting themselves up for an exodus of customers. Who would not want to spend money in an environment that makes them feel like they were worth no more than the value meal on promotion?

For the rest of our time in Ottawa, needless to say, we did not go back to that restaurant. We also did not forget it. While we did not say we would not eat there again, it could be easily concluded that only an adverse circumstance could have led either of us back to that location. We also continued to make the comparison between our experience there and that at Milestones. It was easy to conclude that the servers at Milestones earned way more tips than at this establishment. It could also be concluded that the servers at Milestones were more satisfied with their jobs and it was also very likely that the staff retention rate there was higher. Many other conclusions could be drawn from the comparison of the two experiences. The ultimate conclusion could be that Milestones would be a more profitable operation and likely to survive for a much longer time.

Prescription

- **Know and communicate the type of organization you want to be**

In the entertainment and dining industry, there must be a feature that makes an establishment distinctive. This must be part of the identity of the business. This feature must then drive the success of the organization and must be known, preached and practiced by all employees. If taste is the selected factor, each message must contain some reference to the fact that, barring none, the taste in the establishment was globally the best. It starts with knowing what type of organization you want to be. Strangely, many of the creators of companies did not define at the outset what they would be best known for. With time however, the mega successful organizations were able to create and develop an image which thereafter became a huge part of their success. This restaurant in my view did not seem to have one and the server was just being herself, which likely changed with every customer. While being herself was important, it was more important to be the image of what the organization wanted to present.

Organizational identity would go a long way in etching experiences into the mind of patrons. Milestones achieved that while Scores did not. This could be attributed to the job profile, selection process and training provided to the team members there which in turn influenced the customer experience. I would be surprised if a process as robust existed in the other establishment. Despite the specials, I would bet the annual revenue of Milestones was greater by far. It would be my recommendation to Scores to firstly determine what image they wanted their restaurant to have and build a framework to ensure that all employees understood the intended image and therefore tailor their approach to achieve that. Yes, they could be a low-cost leader but this should not translate into low cost with poor service. It would be no different from Wal-Mart or Sam's Club, where being a low-cost provider did not mean being unfeeling about the customer experience. Once the identity is determined, the investment should be made to have every employee understand it. They should also be trained to understand what is required to live within that corporate image.

Chapter 4 – I will resolve your problem

A few years ago I bought a new laptop computer to replace the one given to my teenage daughter. While I don't claim to be a geek, I do have a reasonable level of understanding about how computers work. After gaining a bachelors degree in information technology, I should be able to relate to simple troubleshooting requirements for a computer. My new laptop was set up and working nicely but for the fact that I needed to get some anti-virus software installed. As was the norm, there was a promotional subscription to one which I was not interested in, and therefore I planned to use Symantec, which I preferred.

After a few days of playing with my new laptop, I was ready to get a subscription for my computer. I had recalled that I could use one Symantec license on three different machines, which was awesome. I logged on to the website with the intention of getting the download, but it was not very clear how to get the second machine protected as each option seemed to suggest that I needed to make a new purchase. My impatience got the better of me and I went ahead and completed the download and install. I was happy that I was able to do it although still somewhat distracted by the idea that I really should not have had to purchase a second subscription. In my disquiet, I began searching the company's website to find a way to get some answers to whether I had done the right thing or not. More importantly, I wanted to see how I could have done it correctly in the first place. I hated to feel as though it was beyond me. Maybe my usually dormant ego had been excited by the situation.

There was a contact option available via chat and I initiated a chat session. The next fifteen minutes included one statement which I will forever remember. An agent acknowledged my request and started the session by stating his name and that he "would resolve my issue". Wow! It was a chat session which limited the ability to transmit the support agents tone. However, with such a profound statement, I could feel positive energy. A culture of care, which was a part of Symantec's support model, was communicated within the first minute. The start of the interaction, which was void of sounds and facial expressions, was so profound that it negated a customer developing negative feelings. This would make the service resolution easier.

In all my sojourns and interactions with support organizations, I had never been greeted in such a profound way before. I had experienced pleasant voices, caring voices, smiles and many other things but never a pronouncement of intent as was the case that day. For those that have used chat applications, they are rather impersonal and the wait for a response from the other participant can often be more than expected. This session was no different. There was a lag in the exchanges and there were times when I wondered if the rep had dozed off. Chances are he felt the same thing about me. With all the limitations which came with the technology that was employed, the way the call started instilled the level of confidence needed to combat the frustration and distant feeling that could have come with the delayed exchanges. I provided information as requested by the agent and he requested permission to manage my desktop remotely. Once that was ongoing, he provided me with a phone number, and took mine, in the event that we lost connection. I did not even think of that but I am sure it was part of the overall operating requirement of that support centre. As we waited for the old application to be uninstalled, I asked him a few questions including where he was located. He was located in India and was nearing the end of his shift. There was no sense of fatigue from the rep which is sometimes the case at the end of a shift. Often, no one wants a customer issue that had more than the average challenge near the end of the day. While it is difficult to tell via the medium we were using, I did not feel that he was less energized than he would have been at an earlier point in the day.

It took us near thirty minutes to remove the program, complete the information required to do a credit and install the appropriate program to my computer. He provided a running commentary on what was happening in each phase and the instructions on what I needed to do, however minimal, was clear. Throughout the interaction, I never had a moment of doubt that he would do as he had said at the start. The apprehension with which I went on the call disappeared quickly. I did anticipate that they may have said there was no refund when customers make silly mistakes and did not read the instructions as they should. I have seen that happen before. Not here. I concluded that I was not the only customer with the disorder and that such occurrences were normal with an established means of resolving them. It made a world of difference that the rep started with the powerful statement which set the tone for the rest of the interaction. My feelings of apprehension, embarrassment and a tinge of fear were quickly substituted with respect and confidence.

In the end my issue was resolved, as the rep had promised, with no hiccups. He was true to his bold promise and earned my respect and trust throughout. In the end, I felt comfortable with the fact that I had made an error and satisfied that he had done what was required to remedy the situation. I also felt that, as a customer, it was worth my time and money doing business with a company like Symantec. If companies are willing to make such bold statements, and live up to them, it inevitably leads to a greater sense of confidence in them. It also demonstrates their recognition, and acceptance, of the importance of customer satisfaction supported by bold steps. During the interaction, it never crossed my mind that the opening line may have been a fancy marketing ploy to mask an environment conducive to sub-par service. It, in my view, was a simple, confident expression by a seemingly well-trained rep which set the stage for an excellent interaction. Prior to the end of our converstaion, the rep advised me that a survey on the quality of the interaction would be sent to me soon after. I confirmed that it would be a pleasure to provide some feedback to his organization on the quality of the service that was provided.

Prescription

- **Create and deliver service in an environment of confidence**

Customer service centres are established to resolve problems. It is very unlikely that a customer service agent typically gets requests that are from customers wanting to provide accolades. The interactions are therefore likely to start with negative feelings, expressions and experiences. The role of the agent is to ultimately do, and say, things which will create a positive feeling within the customer. Where negative feelings existed, these are the targets for transformation. In doing that, there is an enviable skill that is required.

The skill of engaging with the customer, showing empathy, confidence and competence are critical to that process. A key part of that process is the creation and maintenance of an environment which feeds positive feelings. Anything less makes the job of the rep more difficult and the process of transformation takes longer. Imagine the situation where a negative terminology or tone is the platform for a customer service interaction. The likelihood of that interaction moving speedily to resolution is thwarted by the overtones which easily overcome either of the parties involved. I would recommend that all customer service organizations establish within their training and coaching programs, elements which facilitate representatives building their skill in managing the environment in which the work. What may seem like a simple exercise could have tremendous impact on the organization's operations in terms of cost, efficiency and image. The creation of the correct environment reduces the actual time invested in the resolution, which results in increased capacity and higher levels of customer satisfaction.

Chapter 5 – "This is what I do naturally"

Have you ever had one of those customer service encounters that you wished was the norm with all the places in which you did business? From time to time we do have those interactions and while, we would prefer that they did not end, we also use them as benchmarks for future interactions. Our expectations, which, although somewhat unrealistic, appeal to our natural tendency as humans to opt for situations that make us feel good.

I was scanning my bank account online when I noticed a change in the name of one of the savings accounts that I had. While I was not startled, as I recalled some notice about an account change some time back, what got me was the fact that the bank had introduced a new account with a higher interest rate which they did not offer me automatically. I will confess before going further that I am a huge antagonist to the general way banks operate. Their concept of the acceptable spread required to be profitable always leads me to wonder why passing pain to customers was such a standard way to operate. There are fees which are illogical to the simple saver and in essence, you can never really gain too much from basic relationships with banks. I am sure the bankers will have their perspective which may make a lot of sense relative to my fairly emotional perspective. That said, it is one of those institutions that you really cannot live without.

I spent a few minutes on the bank's website looking at the features of the new accounts and the rates being offered. I noticed that there were two accounts with the same name with the distinction of one being tax free (a break by the government). I was a little confused with the offering and decided to call into the customer service line to get some clarification and if possible move my funds to the account with the higher interest rate. Who would not do that? I had every intention of ensuring that the agent was advised of my displeasure with not being offered the appropriate account with the highest interest rates as part of the account name changes. I endured the typical features of the modern corporate phone systems and after pressing a few numbers and entering my account card number, I was connected to a customer service representative. I verified my identity and outlined to the representative the reason for my call. She took some time to explain to me the reason for the change in the account but was somewhat curious as to what action I wanted to take. There were several options which included opening a new account with a higher interest rate, keeping things as they were with the automatic upgrade, or have both the current account and a new account.

We weighed the options and she took the time to outline the different features of all the accounts that we had reviewed. In all this time, she maintained a sense of humour which was catching while at the same time not losing her professional approach. What was interesting to me was, firstly, her acceptance that there could have been a better way of implementing the change, which could have included offering an automatic upgrade to the best product. Secondly, her perspective that there was an opportunity to correct my perception on the call was inspiring my confidence. In the few minutes that we were on the phone we developed a rapport which, for any customer service professional, is a key ingredient to a successful interaction. She understood that although I was not in a rage and expressing negative thoughts, there was a point of dissatisfaction. She was eager to address this, while at the same time gain experience for future interactions of a similar nature. It was likely that other customers would have reactions similar to mine, and she not only became more proficient in dealing with the specifics of the new accounts but she had determined a workable solution to correct the situation and the feeling that I had.

As we got near the end of the call, she asked for a little more of my time to play an automated description of my selection and thereafter to complete a confirmation procedure. Having done all that, we got to the end of the call. She declared that it was her "call of the day" and expressed appreciation for my patience and understanding. Not only did she sound genuine, I could sense that she enjoyed our interaction. I then told her how I felt and that I was impressed with the way she had handled the interaction. She was at a loss for words momentarily as I could hear that my words had struck an emotional chord. I explained that I was in the role of managing a customer service operation and I hoped that all the agents on my team sounded and acted like she had. She knew that I had no reason to flatter her. I was the customer and our physical paths were never likely to cross, so whatever occurred on the call was all that we would have had. What she said next was profound and spoke to the core of what made the experience memorable. She expressed thanks for my kind words and appreciation that I took that time to provide such a compliment. She said that having been in the role for many years, she behaved that way naturally. The care, attention and appreciation of the need to address the feelings of the customer, in addition to solving the problem, had, with time, become a part of her professional fibre. That was the definition of operating normally. In operating that way, she did not need to make any extra effort to deliver exceptional service. Effectively, she had committed to always being exceptional.

After all the exchange and interchange she asked me to log into my account to view the changes. She offered to do a transfer of funds from one account to newly created one. I opted to do it myself; after all, the experience was enough. She had done more than I had asked. I was feeling great about her, her organization and about me. What more could I have reasonably asked of her. I had started the afternoon with every intention of doing the transaction myself once I had received the clarification. Here I was minutes later blown away by a customer service professional at the top of her game. That was not where I had planned on being but I was there and it had worked out well.

Even though my perception of banks did not change, I was prepared to continue as a customer of her organization. I was not planning on moving my business but there was no commitment to staying either. The previous week I had moved money to a new investment opportunity as the returns were better. There was nothing stopping me from doing the same should there have been a reasonable offer. It was commonplace for the suitors to provide numerous incentives and services to make transfers smooth. What this experience did for the organization was to solidify, if only in the short term, my stay as a customer. Who would not want to do business with an organization that was represented that way? The way I felt as a customer would really be no different for the many thousands of other customers. Banks, as with other financial institutions, thrive on the confidence of their customers. At the end of the day, their success is based on how they make their customers feel. It may not always translate into having a naturally congenial, open-minded representative, like the one I interacted with. However, if in the end, the interactions result in positive outcomes, they would have done what was required to retain customer confidence. There is no customer who would not want to have a positive experience which left them feeling good.

Prescription

- **Build on the strengths of your superstars**

Each organization, especially those with national and multi-national reach should ensure they magnify the impact of all their resources to gain and maintain competitive advantage. This should be a strategy for all forward thinking companies. It would be great if the interaction with this representative was recorded, reviewed and utilized for training other representatives. It is a great motivator to teams when the examples of excellence come from within their ranks. While it may sometimes create a little pressure on these individuals to be standard bearers, it could also serve as a recognition tool which motivates these individuals. The benefits that organizations derive from outstanding customer experiences have created many opportunities reflected in the numerous awards being copped annually by those that make the investment to apply. The recognition for their efforts to improve and deliver customer experiences was built on the work of some of the superstars.

Many opportunities exist to build programs, outside of the tacky "Employee of the Month" kind, which allow peer collaboration and leadership on initiatives to deliver and maintain outstanding customer experiences. The employees in the trenches are usually way more capable of influencing their peers than they are often credited. They have the experience to influence the structure of support models that capitalize on their expertise to deliver corporate results.

I will conclude that this bank has excellent training programs for employees at all levels. Notwithstanding, I would also propose that it continues its customer experience improvement by implementing peer driven improvement programs. Such programs would recognize superstar performers, build skill, enhance team relationships and provide management with new options for organizational development.

Chapter 6 – "This is making me work too hard"

It was late Saturday night. I was out on a weekend with the boys. Most of my sojourns had been on my own, so being on a road trip with my friend was very different from what I have normally done. That said, we were having a good time, eating some outstanding meals and just having a laid back time away from the pleasure and grind of being at home with our families. With the freedom came a need to optimize all our hours. Boredom seemed always to be a breath away. Most of the day was spent in a gorgeous park. A long session at the driving range was followed by a round of beer and loose chatting with some cricket buddies. Then came the night. We started the evening at a friend's house. Dinner was great and the topic of discussion moved from music to food and many variants between. Danny, an affable older guy that was there, ensured that there was no lack of entertainment. He recalled numerous stories; some which I am sure were fabricated, about his younger days and all the escapades he had experienced. Inevitably, the conversation continued until the discussion was about women and sex.

His partner, a chubby woman of Italian descent, was quite conservative and at different points was finding the subject and the details a bit much to handle. She went to the bathroom and on returning expressed her tiredness which led to them leaving. We took the cue and left as well. It was just after 10 p.m. and we were in no mood to call it a night. It was our free weekend and our intention was to make the most of it. My buddy called a friend to ask about the different hotspots on a Saturday night. He recommended a club that played our genres of music. We were sorely disappointed when we arrived as there was little action there. A few patrons milling outside may have had the same reservations we did. I was not prepared to pay an admission fee to sit in a club where there was nothing happening. After a few minutes, we opted to leave and check out other places that we had seen along the way. We recalled that there were a few action spots near our hotel. We did not have a chance to assess the style of these spots but agreed to go check them out.

An hour later we were at the entrance to an adult entertainment club. As with the previous stop, we had some reservations but testosterone decided on our behalf and we paid and entered the sparsely populated joint. As expected, the lights were dim and the few patrons were scattered in the many lounge chairs around. No one took the upright chairs in the front row which may have been the reason the lone dancer on the stage seemed somewhat apathetic towards her role. My friend and I settled into the second row lounge seats and were soon being offered drinks by an affable server. She was in her mid twenties, and, judging from her legs, was either an athlete or someone who spent a reasonable amount of time in the gym. She surely understood what was required to make an initial impression. They did not have what I would have preferred to drink; I settled for vodka with ginger while my friend opted for a rum and cola. We laughed at the sizes of the drinks when she returned and suggested that in an establishment of that nature, size should be of greater consideration. The server enjoyed a few moments of hilarity with us before going off to assist other patrons. We both agreed that with her body, she would be a great source of entertainment on the stage. On entry we were told that the main show would have started soon and we sat and sipped on our drinks in anticipation of the action.

As the set of the dancer on stage ended, she strolled with intent towards us. I anticipated the usual offer of private entertainment, as was standard in these clubs. We chatted for a few minutes before she went off to chat with the other patrons. I concluded that she was as bored as we were and was not keen to small talk too much. We endured two other sets of dancers. There was nothing memorable about either and we speculated about the age of a few of the dancers. We chatted about our experience in similar establishments and the expectations that were driven by those experiences. The sexy server came back to check on us and offer a second round of overpriced drinks. The night was moving way slower than either of us would have wanted and, but for the visual pleasure from the server, the night had not delivered on its promise. I couldn't help but wonder if anyone was taking into consideration that there were paying customers who were maybe not feeling the way they would have anticipated. The DJ and dancers were operating in zones that were not in alignment to ours. Maybe our faces and body language did not tell the story.

Having finished her set, another of the dancers ventured our way. She started in the stoic way the others did, almost as if it were a standard greeting that was imposed on them by a regulatory organization. She said her name was Amber and that she wanted to offer me a private dance. I asked her a few teasing questions, trying to get the conversation to a real level and also to see how much she was really into entertaining.

After all, if I was going to spend more money, I wanted to get best value for my investment. I was not trying to buy sexual activity but any spend on safe flirting had to be worth my while. Her responses suggested that she had never had customers who asked the questions I did. For a moment I attributed her attitude to naivety, which was forgivable. A few more exchanges led to a response that was indeed memorable. She smiled and said she was leaving as "this was making me work too hard". I was floored. How could trying to proposition a customer to spend more money on private entertainment in a club that was by no means overflowing with customers be too much work? It was even more startling considering my attempts to flirt with her throughout.

My friend and I sat there laughing at the conclusion which was clearly best for everyone. What it meant was that she did not have to make any additional effort to please us and we did not have to feel cheated of our money, as it was not likely she would have done more to provide us with satisfying entertainment. Having left, I wondered about all the men who had agreed to the solicitations previously. Did they feel satisfied with the services provided or did they leave feeling that there was a sub-par delivery? Granted, they may not have been as conscious as I was about the entire situation. It is understandable that when driven solely by lascivious intent, logic and analysis can be sidelined.

I thought about sharing my opinion with the owner of the club or any of the other dancers. That did not happen as I am sure she made sure her colleagues knew that we were cheap customers who were not willing to play the games to the rules. Understandably, they would have accepted her version and respond to us as we deserved. For the rest of the time we stayed there, we could feel the cloud of scorn over our heads. We finally decided that it was time to leave and proceeded to the exit. As I trailed my partner to the stairs, I overheard our lazy dancer explaining to the guys manning the entrance how boring we were and that we were not prepared to comply with the club rules. I paused for a moment to listen to the conversation before quickly deciding that it was not worth my time. It was unlikely that they would have presented a perspective that balanced the story, especially since it may have been normal to have patrons in the club who did not want to comply with the rules. As we walked to our hotel, which was only a few blocks away, we recounted the situation and what could have been. Our willingness to spend money was swallowed by a shallow perspective which effectively kept money out of that business. Not only the initial spend; but also the loss of repeat business and referrals. The sad thing was that we were convinced that the management would not have seen any deficiency in the approach of their staff.

As I reflected on the experience, I came to the conclusion that no matter what the business venture, the business must be committed to doing their best to deliver on the customers' expectations. Anything less will border on selfishness or apathy being the victor in a battle over addressing the customers' feelings. In this case, the dancer did not care too much how I would have felt leaving that club after her remark. In her mind, she simply stated the way she felt and that should have been fine with me, despite the fact that I was there to add to the revenue of the operation. Additionally, even if I was broke and had no opportunity to spend, I would still want to be treated like a worthy guest. Neither occurred and she did not seem to understand the potential effect of her style. My wandering mind then concluded that the spattering of customers was not because it was an adult entertainment joint but because there were many others like me who were not willing to sacrifice their feelings to feed testosterone driven desires. It must have happened before where one of the ladies was not willing to work too hard to make a customer feel wanted. The consequent action would be to leave and never return. If you were in an establishment were you were not made to feel worthy, you would likely do the same, especially where the services being offered were not immediate necessities.

Prescription

- **Ensure employees earn their customer service credits.**

Each operator of any business that delivers a good or service must establish principles that will govern the operation. In the case of the club, each employee should therefore be trained to offer service with the same zest as they would were they working in a retail store. The behaviours demonstrated a perception built on the nature of the business and the need to be different. In such industries, there is clearly the need to be tough. This should not however change the core principles. All customers are valuable to the operation and should be made to feel that way, even when they are not high rollers. This perspective should start with the ownership and permeate to all involved. I would recommend that the owner spend time explaining the nuances of the business and provide tips on how to be successful.

A great way to generate the type of excitement required

to provide that level of service would be a team rally before the start of each night. As is common in sales teams, a burst of adrenaline within the team environment would transform the negative tendencies into a fun affair which would translate into the confident, sexy behaviour which is a requirement for success in that industry. The owner would also want to coach the ladies based on the behaviours he noticed and also explain the psychology behind men being in the club. If that were understood, the ladies would be more prepared to cater to the needs of the customers, instead of merely resorting to sexually stimulating gyrations. A different approach would guarantee positive feelings and more spending from the patrons. In the process, the owner could also learn more about his customer base and the secrets to more revenue. With these insights, the challenge of creating entertainment for the night and customers for many years, would be made significantly easier.

Chapter 7 – Acknowledge me

It was July and I had the opportunity to be in Jamaica for two weeks. Not only was there the enticing experience of time on a tropical island, I was bereft of my small children and wife. In one way, it was not the ideal summer experience as I would have loved for them, especially my four year old, Danielle, to be part of the vacation, while on the other hand, it was a welcome break from all the familial responsibilities that consumed most of my waking moments. Like all other vacations, I anticipated that the days would pass way faster than my days at work and I was keen to make the most of every moment. When we landed, it was a balmy thirty two degrees Celsius and I was ready for it.

In addition to having to get local currency and collect my rental car, I also needed to purchase a mobile phone. I did have a phone with me, however it was a company issued phone and I was conscious about all the roaming and long distance charges that would accumulate should I use it to stay in touch with home. Purchasing a phone locally was the correct thing to do and I was keen to get it done as quickly as possible as I was sure my daughter would have been eager to chat with me as soon as I got there. Even though she was only four, she had a strong sense of connection, not to mention the natural curiosity that was present at that age. With the available technology, it was a reasonable expectation to ignore the impact of distance on one's ability to stay in touch.

With the car rental and currency exchange completed, I headed for the mobile phone retail outlet to do my next transaction. I was hungry; however that desire took second place to my fixation on getting a phone. In my mind, it should have been a quick transaction which would make it more relaxing to go and have a meal. The store was relatively close to where I did the money exchange so I chose to walk there. When I entered, I was greeted by a pleasant young lady who wore a badge which identified her as "Trainee". I took the liberty to ask if that was her first or last name, which she took in great stride. She offered to assist me in selecting the handset that I wanted and after answering a few questions about the pricing and make of a few handsets, I decided on a brand she had recommended. My intention was to purchase the lowest cost handset available as my need was limited to simple voice or text communications. The phone would have been given to a friend or relative at the end of my vacation. The trainee accompanied me to the counter where the sales were transacted. She asked one of two clerks working behind the counter if the handset she had recommended was available. They were sold out. The trainee apologized for the situation and recommended another handset which she knew was in stock. Even though it would cost a little more, I was ready to make the purchase and consequently joined the line again. There were two persons ahead of me. I could not say what transaction the man at the head of the line was doing but it seemed to be taking quite a bit of time. The clerk was busy entering information into the computer system while waiting impatiently for something to happen. The guy ahead of me was clearly getting a little irritable. He, like all customers, wanted to have his transaction completed with the least investment in time, which I am sure the clerk also understood. Who wouldn't?

As we waited, and the line grew longer, the clerk appeared to be trying different options to get the first gentleman's transaction completed. Her cell phone rang and she promptly answered. She conducted a quick conversation while we watched and listened. I thought it was unacceptably casual for her to have done that but not knowing the nature of the call made it unfair for me to pass judgement on her. In all fairness to her, it did not appear to impede the service being provided to the gentleman. He was the customer getting the attention and that was it. A few moments after she finished her call, a male colleague came to her station and leaned in to whisper something to her. The chatter continued for a few minutes, within full view of all of us standing there. They both had a laugh at what was shared and he left and she returned to the computer to update the gentleman at the front. She spoke to the customer and the wait continued and she turned her attention to counting a wad of money. The man before me asked her a quick question regarding a product. He wanted to know if any was in stock. The distance between them could have been no more than five feet however she continued her counting without even looking at him. He waited and asked again with the same outcome. I was flabbergasted. I could not believe that she did not respond to him. While I could understand her need to concentrate on her immediate task of counting, it baffled me that she could not have attempted to acknowledge the customer's question and communicate her intention to attend to him momentarily. Instead, it was the obvious ambivalence which reflected that she did not really care how it made him feel as her task was way more important than acknowledging the customer.

Needless to say, I decided to leave the store. I was not prepared to spend money in an establishment that treated customers that way. On my way out, I wondered if she had even noticed that I was in the line. As I crossed the street *en route* to my car, I wondered if she saw me leave and what were her thoughts. It would have been likely that she thought "happy riddance", another customer that would be easily replaced and she may have been right. Strangely, I felt a sense of relief leaving the store. I felt like I did what the man before me should have done. He was the one that was not acknowledged. However, I did feel unwanted and even though she may have treated me differently, I could not find it within me to think better of her. From what she had demonstrated in the near thirty minutes that I stood there, it was unthinkable that she would have been any different. Chances are, considering the frustration she may have been experiencing, I may have been up for some unpleasant service.

The entire episode reinforced to me the desire of every customer to be acknowledged and being busy is no excuse for missing the opportunity to recognize the presence of a person. Before being a customer, we are all persons and would like to be accepted and recognized accordingly. This is equally important as businesses attempt to grow their revenue and customer base. If one customer is treated in a particular way, there is the tendency to close ranks and defend that customer. In some cases, the response is an expression of protest, as was the case in this situation. In other cases, there are vocal responses while in others there are written comments. This could all have been avoided, there could have been additional revenue for the company and the opportunity for repeat business, if there was a simple acknowledgement of a customer. When expressed in this way, it is logical to question if the clerk looked at her lack of positive action, in the same way. If the answer is yes, there is the chance of her recognizing the fault and correcting it on the next occasion, while to the contrary, she could continue behaving in the same way until it reached a crescendo and she was terminated.

As I drove away that day with my hurt feelings and full wallet, I pondered on the potency of effective eye contact and body language in customer interactions. While for some it may be an exaggeration of simple actions, for others it was the difference between feeling important and being treated as invisible.

Prescription

- **Make respect a basic employment criterion**

I concluded after thinking about it long and hard that the root cause of the experience in the store was a lack of basic respect. Whether we want to quote Confucius or the Bible, there was the absence of a basic tenet of treating others the way you would want to be treated. I am in no way suggesting that all customer facing organizations be built on religious beliefs. Some, like me, would scoff at the idea. It is however important that an organization be driven by principles which are grounded in the culture of the company. Some basic requirements must exist for being invited to join the organization and also key to being allowed to remain with the entity. Without being draconian, there is need, especially when the interactions are many and varied, for the managers of the organization to ensure that these tenets are reinforced and practice. Practice facilitates the formation of habits.

For this company, my recommendation would be two-fold; have managers assess the degree to which clerks display behaviours which reflect respect for the customers. They should also include greater rigour in the recruiting process to focus on the applicants' perception of respect and customer value. Often, people exhibit behaviours that they consider acceptable, when, if examined in a different context, could be perceived otherwise. Unfortunately, there is not always an opportunity for self examination, or coaching, and these practices continue until they become commonplace. Customers form their perception of an organization based on the behaviours displayed by employees. It is amazing how within a few interactions that image is formed and solidified. Effective and decisive management can quickly shape the practices to achieve the desired outcomes.

Chapter 8 – Going the extra mile

It was my first tradeshow and while I did not outwardly show it, I was really excited. In my previous roles, the opportunity did not arise for me to participate in such events. Not only would I get to visit a new city, I would also get to see how customers, critics and competitors responded to our product showcase. This event had always been a huge investment for the company as it was the largest showcase of its kind in North America, our strongest market. The flight was uneventful and the warmth of California greeted us the moment we hit the terminal building. It was a welcome break from the cooler climate that we were accustomed to. Our group was large and one of the vice presidents suggested we all ride together in the rental van he had reserved. With all the bags, and the best intentions, we all could not fit. Another guy said he would rent an additional vehicle and I opted to ride with him. At least there would be a bit more comfort. I had already loaded my bag into the van but thought little of the fact that we would be separated for a while. It would have been only a few minutes before I would get to the hotel and collect it.

The trip from Los Angeles to Anaheim where we were booked to stay was not as scenic as I had expected. It is strange how we conjure images of different places based on what we see and hear about these places. For me, California, and Los Angeles specifically, was supposed to have manicured lawns, grandiose beaches and blondes in Ferraris everywhere.

Unfortunately, it was just another city. We arrived at our hotel and headed for the check-in. I had not had a reasonable meal all day and was in need of some food. My goal was to quickly find my bag, get to my room and then to the nearest restaurant to resolve my hunger. Then my challenges started. I did not see any of the colleagues who were on the van which had my bag. I assumed that in unloading all the bags, someone had taken my bag and placed it in safekeeping. I therefore went directly to check-in. The check-in clerk advised me that there was no reservation for me at that hotel. That was surprising. I made a call to the coordinator of the event who advised that due to my late confirmation, I was booked at a hotel about fifteen minutes away. The hotel was fully booked due to the tradeshow and the other activities in the area. The colleague I had travelled with suggested I take the rental car, as he was based at the hotel and had no real need for it. I then started the search for my bag.

I was not sure where to start so I started with the elegantly dressed guy, Juan, at the concierge desk. He did advise that a party arrived in a van bearing the descriptions I had given but that he did not recall them leaving a bag there for me. With that response, I figured that more specific information on what they had done with my bag would have made it easier to find it. I called one of my colleagues who was in the van who told me that she was sure all the bags were removed from the vehicle but had no idea where it had been left. After a few calls to other colleagues who were on the van, I was no closer to finding my bag. It was now nearly an hour later and no one had been of much help. I went back to the concierge desk and explained my plight further to an attentive Juan. He suggested that I look in the baggage storage area, even though I did not have a ticket to reconcile with my lost bag. He hinted that it may have been placed there without a tag, even though it should not have been. Off I went to search. I went up and down the rows several times pulling tags to see if my name was on them. In retrospect, it is interesting how the mind works. In the quest for a glimmer of hope you ignore the facts standing in front of you. My bag as a black leather pull-on and here I was looking at mixed coloured, larger bags – just in case. I did this for way longer than I should have until I finally went back to Juan to share my disappointment. He commiserated with me and suggested that it may have been placed in the long term storage area and he offered to search that area. Juan said he had been at the hotel for many years and could not recall a bag being lost. He was confident that it would be found. While I appreciated his optimism, I was still baffled by its disappearance and the fact that no one who was in the van, at least the ones I had spoken to, had seen anything of my bag. I told him I was rather hungry and while I was a trifle frustrated, I would be best served with something to eat. He took my phone number and recommended one of the restaurants on the property and promptly provided me with directions. He promised to search the main area again and also the long term storage section while I was gone.

I found the restaurant. Some of my colleagues who had travelled in the van were also there. They queried whether I had found my bag. On telling them that my bag was nowhere to be found, despite all my searches, there were suggestions of places that I could go to get some replacement clothes and personal items. There was a discount department store within walking distance. Strangely, I had not given up on the chances of finding my bag. It was getting late but somewhere inside me, there was a thought that, unless it fell from the van on the highway, it had to be in the hotel somewhere. With that in mind, I joined in the consumption of cocktails. I would have done that anyway and would not allow a slight change in process to deter me. For the next ninety minutes I mingled, laughed and ate with the thought of my lost bag popping into my head ever so often. I wondered if it was being opened by an unsuspecting woman who chose to wander through it searching for something sexy; or by a male who was so disgusted at having a misplaced man's bag in his room that he flung the contents uncaringly on the floor. While I remained calm, clearly there was some anxiety in me.

Near the end of the cocktail period, I thought it would be good to make another attempt at finding my bag. Just as I was about to leave the restaurant, my phone rang and it was Juan calling to advise that despite a search in both the regular and long term storage areas, there was no sign of my bag. I told him I was on my way back to the front of the hotel and when I got there we could look at what alternatives existed. The short walk felt longer than it should have. I was prepared to make the trip to the department stores as I had to be ready for the meetings the next day and the jeans and polo shirt I was wearing would not meet the requirements. I arrived at Juan's station and started discussing the situation. I asked if I could check the main storage area one last time. He said sure and accompanied me inside. Most of the bags were gone which made it a shorter sojourn, but even more definitive. With that done, he said he would make a second search in the long-term storage area, even though he was confident that it was not there. It was near 8 p.m. which was the end of his shift. He took nearly twenty minutes to do the search and came back with the disappointing answer. With no regard to the fact that his shift had ended, he started making phone calls to other members of staff who were in the reception area earlier that day. He quizzed them for suggestions on where else he could possibly look to find my bag. At one point, I said to him that I will accept the loss and go get some clothes at the store nearby. He asked for a few minutes to ask a few more persons as they may have seen it. He was more convinced than I was that there was something odd about the loss and it provided some sense of hope. He suggested that he make one last search in the storage area downstairs from where we sat. He could not have invited me to share in the search as it was a restricted area. For the next twenty minutes I waited patiently at the desk. Juan's relief had arrived and was settling in for his shift. I explained to him what had happened and he assured me that I was in the best possible hands to solve the issue. Soon I saw Juan coming towards us with a huge smile on his face and my black, leather pull-on in his hand. He explained that he searched all the areas a second but this time opted to look in the most unlikely place, his manager's office, where my bag was sitting quietly on the floor. There was no need for an explanation as to how it got there. What difference would it have made? He had spent almost an extra hour of his own time walking around looking for my bag. Neither words nor the tip I gave him could have adequately expressed my gratitude for the effort that he made. With his shift coming to an end, he could have easily done his closing routines and head home. He did not. For him, the investment of a few more minutes to help someone, who was not even a guest at his hotel, was worth it. My sojourn through multiple emotions was culminated with a deep sense of gratitude and appreciation. While he may not have done when dealing with a customer, limits that opportunity to add a "wow" factor that leads to additional business. I would recommend that organizations encourage employees to find, and capitalize, on opportunities to regularly go beyond customer's expectations.

Chapter 9 – Keep your promise

I had the great fortune of being allotted some shares in a company that was going public. The company had developed a market leading position over two decades of operation. The market, and many others, was excited about the prospects of the company and I was grateful to have been given such a special opportunity. There were others, who I am sure would have wanted to have been in my position. With the acquisition of the shares came the need to be more financially aware. While I was no novice to financial matters, I knew it was imperative that I sought the requisite advice quickly in order to effectively capitalize on the situation I was in. After a few days of soaking in my fortune, I called my bank to make an appointment to see a financial advisor. That to me was the logical first step. I explained to the person who had taken my call, that in addition to reviewing my accounts, I needed to sell some of the shares that I had acquired. An appointment was made to meet with a representative at the branch near my home. I was pleased that I had taken the first step towards a more structured approach to investing and I gathered all the paperwork that I thought would have been necessary, including my share certificate, and off to my I appointment I went.

The branch was rather busy that day and I was forced to wait a few minutes past my scheduled time. The representative I was booked to see came out, greeted me and advised that there would be a slight delay. I read a few articles of the ceiling level showing real time market data on seemingly all the financial markets in the world. At the time I arrived, there was a public investment seminar going on. The operation looked impressive. After looking around for a few minutes, a male employee offered to assist me. I told him what I needed and gave him the paperwork that I had carried. He wrote a few things then asked for the complete set of documents that I had received having opened my trading account. I had to retrieve them from my car which I did quickly. Then I asked if he was able to complete the trade on my behalf. He said that he would not have been able to do it as he had to send all the information he had written to their main office before I would be able to start trading. I was starting to feel a bit frustrated. What appeared to be a simple procedure was becoming rather complex. I was already in the process which also made me feel hamstrung. There were not too many options available so I asked how long before I would be able to trade and he advised that it would be a day or two, which was fine with me.

While I was not overly impressed with the service, I left thinking I had made some progress. I had taken a loan to secure the share allocation and was obliged to repay the loan in a few weeks. I had always been prompt in meeting financial obligations and in this case, that was my plan. It was important to me that I paid on time. The sale of the shares would have provided me with that satisfaction and the maintenance of my reputation. None of the representatives I had spoken to was aware of this. In my view that would not have been a part of the conversation anyway. All I really wanted to get was some advice and a trade done. I walked back to my car thinking about how distant my experience with the last representative had been and wondered how he thought I felt during and after our interaction. I wondered also if he correlated that with the growth of his client base and overall business. He may have, just as he may not have. He did take the relevant information to pass to the appropriate sources which was all he could do for me. His tasks were done.

After waiting for a few days, I noticed that my holdings were listed in my account. I was happy that I was now finally able to get going in my own stock portfolio (clearly exaggerated). After several unsuccessful attempts to place a sell request, I called the support line to ask what had been causing the errors I was getting. All seemed correct to me and I was sure I was the legal owner of the shares. Novice that I am, I was still thinking that I had not declared something which was causing these errors. I was also remembering the solemn look on the face of the guy who had taken my information and wondered if his sadness, or whatever his demeanour projected, had resulted in an error. The very pleasant rep on the phone advised that although the holdings were showing in my account, it could take up to another ten days before I could actually trade. He explained the cross market registration process and a few other legal procedures. I explained to him that I needed to execute a trade urgently. While he could not speed up the process, he promised that he would set an alert on my account to have someone, maybe himself, call me as soon as the account was free of the holds. He reiterated my value to their organization and confirmed the best way to contact me. I took comfort in the commitment.

Once off the phone I had to speak to the loan coordinator about my predicament. While he said he would give me a few days to deliver my repayment cheques, he was somewhat sceptical of my reason. I was merely repeating what the brokerage firm's representative had told me, even though, like him, I wondered why it would take that long. I did explain to him that in the event that it took longer than reasonable, which it already had, I would secure another way to repay the loan. I appreciated that he did not make it uncomfortable for me, but I did feel like I had short-changed the lender. I also felt that all along the way, no one at the brokerage took the time to understand my situation and needs. That said, I was now holding on to the promise from the last interaction to finally set my mind at ease.

Three days went by and there was no call. In that time, I checked my online account everyday to see if my stocks were released to facilitate my trade. After the third day I started to be concerned. Yes, the rep had said it could have taken up to two weeks which I was still struggling to accept. On day five, I conceded to my curiosity and checked my account again. My holdings were no longer restricted and I was able to get past the error that had been popping at me all the times before. After a few attempts, including a password change and a call to the support line, I was able to place an order. There was a sense of relief, as I was closer to meeting my obligation and restoring my peace of mind. In the moment of positive feelings, it dawned on me that no one had called to advise me that I was now able to trade. Not that it made a difference, but I started to sum up all the experiences I had with the organization and the sum of negative emotions. Yes, the agents on the telephone were polite and the information on the website was accurate, however my feelings towards the institution were not overly positive because more times than not, I left with a sense that no one was caring too much about my expectations. The perception was merely compounded by the fact that no one called me back as promised. My thought was that she did not make the note on the account as she said she would have. And, should I give her the benefit of that doubt, clearly the reminder did not trigger the appropriate action.

My trade eventually settled and I was able to honour my debt. Even as I wrote the cheques I wondered about the experiences of colleagues that had initiated the same process. In some cases that I was aware of, their trades went without a hitch. The institutions that provided them with the service would have maintained or improved their rating in their eyes and it was likely that they felt like deserving customers. I, on the other hand, was thinking that maybe for my next trades I should look at a new brokerage organization which would be more caring of my needs as a customer and act accordingly. If the representative had not promised to call me, I would have left the interaction accepting that I needed to do my own follow-up to complete the transaction. With the promise came a heightened expectation which was not fulfilled. There was an opportunity to redeem some of the sub-par offering of previous representatives. This was not capitalized on. My reality was that my expectation was not met. While the intentions of the representative were noble and should be commended, the judgement applied to the service provided by an organization is based on the service delivered not the service intended. This case was no different.

Prescription

- **Ensure that the customer's need is known**

The main principle of having a support team is to provide

solutions to customers' problems. In establishing these teams, great care is made in developing the correct profile for the roles and selecting appropriate individuals to perform the tasks. These investments are expected to provide favourable returns and an asset called goodwill to corporations. It is critical therefore that a central theme be established as part of all training and operational initiatives to ensure that representatives understand the customer's need. It is very easy for well intentioned team mates to contribute negatively to an organization because they are so keen on offering support that little time is spent identifying, validating and understanding the customer's need.

In my experience with this brokerage house, my need was defined as the generic requirement of all other customers that fit my profile; that is, a customer with a few shares they wanted to sell. I was not a real investor. If someone had taken the time to identify my need, the conclusion may have been the same without the trappings of negative feelings that came with the different interactions that occurred with the institution. I would recommend that this organization, and all that are serious about world class service quality, instil within their support teams the significance of understanding the customer's need. Their roles are built on understanding the customer's need. Anything less would limit their potential to offer extraordinary service.

Chapter 10 – "We need customers to come back"

It is near 8 o'clock in the evening and I am early into my shift as a volunteer at the casino. Local non-profit organizations receive valuable funding from the provincial government for providing volunteers at the casinos. While the hours were by no means attractive, the benefits derived made that thought disappear quickly. One of the perks of being a volunteer was the opportunity to dine for free while on duty. All the volunteers that I knew made sure to have a hearty meal while there, after all, it did not happen every day.

I needed water, as did other volunteers, which led me to the cafe nearest to our station. As I walked in, the server stopped her tasks and came over to ask me what I was looking to get. She saw my name tag which identified me as a volunteer. Unless she was new in the role, she would have been aware that items ordered by us were placed on our tab and deducted from the allocation made to our association for our work at the casino. I told her I needed to get four bottles of water. Normally, as was the case at other casinos in the city, beverages would have been placed in the volunteer lounge which would negate the need for the trip I had made. In a rather matter of fact way, she stated that she had only one bottle of water left in the cooler. I anticipated that there would have been an offer to get the additional bottles however, her sentence stopped there. They were scheduled to be open for another five hours which begged the question regarding getting a replacement stock of water. For a moment I waited for the additional statement from her and with none forthcoming, I opted to go to another location to get the water. It was clear that she was not inclined to make any effort to get the items for me. I concluded that she may have considered volunteers to be freeloaders and was not prepared to do anything special for them. I had no idea what her thoughts were, but I felt a bit underserved. I briskly walked away to the next food location in my line of sight.

I entered the dining area through what looked like the exit. There were a couple of patrons sitting in the far corner where the light was rather dim. I wandered towards the bar area even though there was no one there. The bar area had lots of color, high stools and, as I presumed, would be the area to attract the attention of the servers. A smiling young lady approached and asked what I needed. My answer was surely not what she was expecting as I questioned whether or not she was prepared to handle some or all of my needs. In a sociable, professional way, she channelled the conversation where she intended while maintaining her smile. She served me the four bottles of water that I was after and queried if that was all I wanted. I was struck by the warmth of her personality and the dramatic difference in the approach compared to the experience I had less than ten minutes earlier. Instinctively I thought that this was somewhere I would have wanted to hang out for a while to continue the warm experience. As I started moving away, I asked about their dinner menu and promised to be back to enjoy more of the top class service that they offered. In my mind, the food there had to be good to support the excellent service that was being provided. Not that I was naive to think that it was a natural correlation. My tendency, however, was to gravitate towards persons and environments which made me feel good. This was one of them.

For the next two hours, I endured what was a boring night in the volunteer booth. I reflected on the experiences in the two establishments and wondered about the mentality of each of the persons I had encountered. I wondered about their lives outside of work, their education, their income and other factors which in my mind could have contributed to their outlook and behaviour. There could have been so many other factors examined but I stopped and focussed on my volunteer tasks until it was time for dinner.

Dinner was fantastic. I opted to have one of the specials on offer which consisted of chicken in a curry sauce with a mix of vegetables and fruits. What seemed like a strange mix of ingredients turned out to be a very delightful dish. After consuming the main course, I remained seated with the thought of having dessert. When the server came back, I reminded her that I had kept my promise from earlier in the evening and I wanted to ask her a few questions. For a split moment she seemed hesitant, likely dreading the line of the conversation I was going to initiate. It was likely that countless other men had seen her beauty and dived in with a heavy flirt. I told her that I was in the process of writing a book on customer service experiences and found hers to be a memorable one which would likely end up in my writings. I discovered that her name was Katie. She was a 24 year-old budding artist with a passion for jewellery with a twist. She had a few visible piercings, including a tongue ring and dressed with an edge. For the next thirty minutes we talked about her experience, her career plans and the reason she was so good at what she did. I discovered that she was in university studying art and held the job at the casino as a means of covering her bills. She had grown up locally and had always been involved in customer contact roles.

Our exchange was very enlightening as I made mental notes of her answers. In the end she said that it was sad when someone in a customer service role did not treat the customer well. She said, *"we always want the customer to come back"*. There is was; the reason she was so good at what she did. She had developed a mantra for her professional life and made an effort to make it happen to the extent that it became second nature. What she also demonstrated was an understanding of the basics of business. Successful businesses revolve around satisfied customers. In situations where there are options, the focus on ensuring customer satisfaction needed to be even higher. The impact of repeat business cannot be overstated. All owners and employees should ensure that the significance of that key equation was understood.

As our conversation continued, Katie told me about her love for art, her desire to develop a new line of jewellery and the potential of new forms of art. From the visible piercings you could deduce that Katie was a girl who lived on the edge and took artistic license for her actions. The foundations that she was creating through the service industry would translate well into her artistic career. She explained that the connections that she made with customers did not only provide for a good tip but also inspired some of the work that she had done. There was an outcome from human connection that appealed to her and influenced her simple approach to people and her job.

I was at the casino for another four hours and reflected constantly on the conversation with Katie. For the rest of the night I was more pleasant with the casino's customers than before. It was an energy gained through the osmosis that occurred with Katie. She would have moved on to another customer with little understanding of how the interaction, and service, she provided made me feel. She had done what was a normal to her. There was therefore no need to wonder about the impact she may have had on me, or any other customer for that matter. I was just another customer that she had treated well with the hope that I would return to their location on another day. If all servers took the approach she did, the economies in many cities and towns would be stimulated by the stream of return customers that would spend time in their businesses. This establishment was fortunate to have an employee with this level of customer care and focus.

Prescription

- **Make customers king of the operation**

All successful businesses operate on the principle of earning more than is spent. While this may appear simplistic, it is the fundamental basis for financial success. It also is the basis on which an organization is able to finance its growth in a fiscally responsible way. It is critical therefore that the key components of the success equation are known and communicated within an organisation. One component of the success equation, that must be established, is the premier role of the customer. It is also critical that the equation does not change as the organization gets bigger and more successful. It is not uncommon for organizations to lose their identity and change their success formulae. In some cases, the significance of the customer diminishes. In many other cases the changes are not formally communicated but occur through other strategic initiatives which change the focus of employees.

In the midst of lack of clarity, it is not uncommon for different, personal styles to come to the fore which may not be reflective of what the business's success equation is. It then becomes even more important that organizations make it a key part of their operational strategy to constantly reinforce, through operational and strategic actions, that the customer will eternally be king of the operation. This could be achieved through various means, including training sessions, mission statements, pep talks and formal executive led communications. For this organization, it would be great if all employees were taught the simple line that Katie stated to me. The simplicity, yet profound nature of the statement, would resonate with employees at all levels. There was also the option of creating signs within the establishment which reinforced to employees, while communicating to customers, what the *modus operandi* of the business was. Any method of ensuring that employees, and customers, knew the company's perspective of the customer would provide positive outcomes.

Chapter 11 – "I have to treat you good"

You would have to see this operation to believe that it operated successfully for nearly twenty years. It was not the typical storefront that one would see in a developed country. It had no sign, no attractive building, nor a chair that you could rest on. There was no business card or keepsake available to show a friend that you were likely to share your experience with. It was one of those non-descript operations which had a simple approach which lead to a success story – treat each customer in a special way.

I was in Jamaica for a visit and after dusk had set in, my uncle, like myself, felt a bit hungry. We did have dinner but, as was the case when the relaxation of vacation kicks in, we were hungry to have more of the authentic local cuisine. At that hour, the traditional eateries were closed and the ones that weren't did not have the menu that was attractive for that hour of the day. He suggested that we get some fried fish and bammies (a thick wafer made from cassava). I was not aware of where we could have gotten such fare at that time. He knew. He was clearly more aware of the happenings in the area than I was. I had only been there for a few days and had rarely gotten out in the evenings. Within a few minutes we were driving along the sparsely lit road to the town centre. We were only a mile away and having driven on the road hundreds of times; it was easy to safely manoeuvre past the many potholes that existed. Soon we saw the lights of the town centre. As we got nearer, my niece who had accompanied us said, "I can see smoke, that means she is there" which was a little confusing to me. I queried what she meant and she explained that the place we were going was open. Once there was smoke in the air, it was confirmation that the food we were looking for was available.

It was Friday and the buzz around the town center reflected the acceptance that the work week was almost over and people were in the mood to relax. There was activity everywhere; from the average worker who was hanging out and having a few drinks with his friends, to the single mother hustling to get home via a local taxi whose operator was in no real hurry to take her home. After searching for a convenient parking spot, we walked towards the smoke that my niece had referred to. Once there the story unfolded. In the midst of a small gathering was a short, slightly rotund lady, Madgie, who was busily moving between two large fire pits. In one pit was a collection of breadfruits being roasted while in the other was a large frying pan filled with fish. Somewhere between both fires she had a few tables on which she stored everything she needed for the operation; pots, wrapping paper, serving plates and more. Under the table she had a few coolers filled with drinks, more fish and other supplies. She was clearly an expert at multi-tasking, as confirmed by the ease with which she moved between the different tasks while having light chatter with all the persons gathered around. She acknowledged everyone that stood there and knew exactly what each person had ordered.

Being new to the operation I stood on the outskirts until she asked me what I wanted. We were planning to order a large amount of food, which was more than what the standard order looked like. I told her that we would wait for the next round of food from the frying pan as we wanted lots more than was currently ready. She dived into some local humour and said she would have my items ready in a short time. The ease with which she engaged us diverted my focus from the less than ideal setting. In other jurisdictions, it would have been an unacceptable way to operate a food establishment. In spite of all the activities she was doing simultaneously, she did not miss a beat in engaging different customers with a smile. In her inimitable way, she made sure that the wait was pleasurable and seemingly shorter than it actually was.

Eventually, it was our time to be served. The fresh smell of recently fried fish filled our lungs as she prepared our order in front of our eyes. There was still a buzz from the fresh olive oil dripping from the fish as she packaged it. We waited as she sliced the bammies and breadfruit that would also be fried for us. Yes, we enjoy fried foods especially when on holidays in Jamaica. When all was done and Madgie calculated our bill, there was no hesitation to pay whatever she stated. I told her that I was impressed with the food we had packaged and that I was eager to get home to get into it. She continued to laugh as part of the exchange and gave me an extra fish and a slice of bammy to eat right there. It was as if she was tipping me for making such a large purchase. We said goodbye and thanked her for the wonderful food she had provided, she laughed and stated that she had to "treat us good". That was the colloquial way of not only expressing gratitude but also a sincere commitment to making the customer feel special. She had clearly done that for many patrons for many years.

While it was my first experience purchasing food from Madgie's stall, I was impressed; not only with the food, but also with the concept of service that was at the heart of the operation. There was no sophistication to the way things were structured; in fact, some aspects were primitive by normal standards. The fact that it lacked sophistication did not affect either the operator or the client base. She was able to attract clients from all strata of the society and impress them with the customer service basics that would be enviable for more established businesses. I am not aware of whether she was able to effectively do the accounting for her business but I would imagine that in the same simple way that she shifted efficiently from task to task, there was a method to how she had successfully operated her food service for over a decade. It had been the source of her income which educated her kids and provided her with an honest livelihood.

There was a steady stream of repeat consumers that ensured that she continued to grow her business. After reaching home and thoroughly enjoying more than my fair share of the items, I asked my niece a few questions about Madgie's business. She informed me that it had been operating like that for many years. Weekends were when many families made her food the "take-out" of choice. It was great that, no matter what the weather, there was always the expectation that she would be there and always offered the same smiling service that we had witnessed earlier in the day. It was revealed that there were times when the operation was so busy that the wait time would be almost an hour to get the desired items. Despite the wait, no one left without fulfilling their order and Madgie never forgot the order in which customers were to be served.

It is not often that small, owner operated businesses are able to grow their clientele with the simplicity applied by Madgie. Often there are programs operated by municipal governments or non-profit organizations geared towards making the path for small entrepreneurs more structured. No such program or opportunity existed in this case. I would hazard a guess that Madgie was functionally literate and not likely to have considered finding such a program to help grow her business. A wave of common sense, and respect for humans, emanated from the operation which reflected the heart of the operator more than anything else. There was no overtone of theory learned in business school. She had developed her business philosophy from the lessons learned through the hard knocks of a challenging lifestyle. Her principles were built on the instinct of survival and the utilization of some very basic skills that improved with time. It culminated in a solution that produced amazing results and was worthy of documentation.

For the next week, we chose to visit her several times. With each visit, the admiration of what she did left a warm feeling within. While, in her view, she was merely offering food and a taste of local culture, she was offering a palatable experience that would touch the core emotions of all her customers. As she had said to me and countless others, a big part of her operation was to make people feel good about themselves while patronizing her business. It could have been a mere transaction, however, that was transformed into a memorable experience that warranted multiple repeat visits because of the strong impact it had, not only on the palate, but also on the person.

Prescription

- **Caring is part of the service offering**

There are many lessons to be learned from the experience with

Madgie that could form part of a customer service curriculum. One key component would be the tremendous value that caring contributes to the service quality of an organization. It could be argued that employees may not have the same personal commitment to an organization's success as the owners and, there would be great validity to that position. There is the need however, for any representative of an organization to be responsible for sharing the values of the organization with every customer. In sharing these values, the genuine commitment displayed will reflect the care factor being discussed.

Every customer wants to feel that their business, or interaction, with an entity is valued. The response of whoever is delivering that service is what will be measured to determine how the organization feels. While not always a fair way to measure an organization, there are no other simple options to the customer. This is where each employee plays a crucial role in shaping the customers' perception of the organization. This dynamic should be explained to all employees. In doing this, without requiring owner style mentalities, employees are asked to operate within the bounds of their humanity and deliver service on a principle of caring. I would prescribe this to all organizations, especially those where personal interactions are the norm.

There is also the need for the establishment of an environment that typifies caring and where owners, managers and non-management employees respect the creed of the organization and practice this. In doing this, the culture is solidified and the care meted out is not artificial. The existence of this feature internally makes it easier to diffuse it outwards. The care factor must start, and live, within the organization in order for it to be felt by the customer.

Chapter 12 – Wrong impression

During my wife's pregnancies with our two daughters, I assumed the task of going to the grocery store. I will admit that there were personal motives behind the decision. I was determined to get the shopping done quicker. My wife tended to walk down every aisle, look at things that were not on the shopping list and occasionally engage in passing conversations with strangers. As her mobility decreased, I took over the shopping and was able to speed through the process. I was also able to determine the time of day that it was done. My preference was usually early in the morning just when the store opened. In my mind, not only would there be limited traffic at the time, there would also be fresh fruits and vegetables and the chance to have the rest of the day unaffected by the shopping trip.

Our grocery store had gone high-tech and had installed self-serve stations which allowed customers to scan their items and complete the check-out process unassisted. I loved the idea as I was not always in the mood to join the line to the cashier or engage in light chatter while she checked our groceries. One Saturday, the self-serve stations were not functional which forced everyone to line up for the cashiers. Like other customers, I looked for the shortest line. As I pushed my cart past one of the check-out lines, I made eye contact with a cashier who suggested that I join her line as she would soon be done with the customers already in line. There was no real reason to doubt her and for a moment I wondered if there was some incentive for her cashing out more customers. How often do you get someone asking for more work if it could be avoided? I had seen her before but never thought to go to her as she always seemed grumpy and unfriendly. While standing in the line, I had an opportunity to see her at work and was forced to rethink the impression that I had formed from previous observations. She appeared versed at what she did and displayed a deep care for each customer she served. I had a cart that was way over capacity which meant I would be there longer than all the customers that she had helped earlier. The next twenty minutes changed my view of her and that store.

From the moment I started unpacking, Lucy, I learnt her name from her name tag, started making the standard offers. Did I want shopping bags? No. Did I find all the things that I had on my list? Yes. From the size of my shopping cart I would have suggested that there may have been even more than I had planned to buy. She also took time to tell me about the things that were on special. In the process she confessed that it was a requirement of the job and that I should not be annoyed as, clearly I appeared to have gotten the things I was looking for. The person I had considered to be the ogre of the store was the chirpiest person on the planet. She expeditiously checked-out my items and once she was done, advised me to go to a nearby refrigerator to collect a bonus item which was given to all customers with purchases over a certain amount. It was interesting that she did this. I had not presented a coupon which is the normal way that the bonus items were usually issued. Without being prompted, she explained that she always tried to work in the interest of the customer and ensured that they were aware of the bonus items on offer, and automatically got them, once eligible. "I always do that for my customers and they always like coming back to me", she stated in her raspy voice. I will admit that my perspective was being transformed with each moment as I would never have drawn those conclusions about her. These were things she was saying about herself with a great deal of confidence. There was no reason to blow her own trumpet. She was merely being genuine about how she saw her role in the store.

She completed my transaction, bade me goodbye and moved on to the next customer. While I packed the groceries, I listened to her have meaningful conversations with a few customers in a very personalized way. Clearly, her claim that customers came back to her was holding true. As she had done for me, she did the routine promotions but also volunteered help to the customers. I left the store with a positive feeling about the store and the overall service experience. I did not expect that and, had the self-serve lanes been operational, Lucy's charm would have been given to someone else. What could have been another normal, mundane day at the store was enhanced by the effort Lucy made to making me feel that she cared and wanted to contribute positively to my shopping experience.

My routine for grocery shopping changed thereafter. Each time I shopped, I checked to see if she was there and was more than willing to wait in her line to share the service experience she provided. From the length of the lines going to her relative to other cashiers, it was true that customers came back to have her check-out their groceries. There may have been other reasons that she had line-ups each time, but it was very likely that some customers were in search of another memorable shopping experience by having her contribute positively to their day. For the many times that I went to her, she remained consistent in her approach and never failed to do the basics and make me feel like she was looking out for me and all the other customers. One day I was a few dollars off to qualify for the bonus item; that day it was a new cordless phone. She suggested that I go get another item to make me eligible. As I was taking off to do that, she apologized to the customers in line and advised them that she really wanted me to get the bonus item. That was sweet. I scampered back and continued the process. She was seemingly more pleased than I was that I was able to get the item.

As our children grew up, my wife regained control of the grocery shopping which took away my usual engagement with Lucy. On the odd times that I would go to the store to pick up a few items, I would look to see if she was there offering her trademark experience. I always recalled the fact that my initial impression was based on a very cursory view of her and what she did. Once I had the opportunity to get a personal experience, that perception was quickly erased and replaced by one that was more accurate and appealing. It did lead me to think that there are many individuals in service roles that are ambivalent to the fact that impressions are constantly being formed which affect the way customers interact with their business. It could be successfully argued that in many cases the conclusions drawn are built on shallow, if any, foundations. It does not however change that fact that impressions are made and perceptions are influenced. In many situations there are simple ways to correct these perceptions. Correcting them may limit the potential financial fallout where negative perceptions exist. That is not always the case, which makes it important that those providing customer service make efforts to provide positive, lasting impressions. It is equally important to be genuine in the delivery of service as the expectations of the customer will the either stay the same or increase. Each time I went grocery shopping I expected Lucy to be chirpy and helpful. Anything less would be below par, leading to questions about what happened to change the standard of service being provided. Service standards are crucial to maintaining customers. Imagine if every time you bought coffee at your favourite coffee shop that it tasted different, even though you ordered the same thing. The likely outcome would be a change in your purchasing pattern in order to achieve the consistent taste that you desired. In the end, while there is significant power in the "wow factor" from an initial experience, real lasting power comes from the residual value of consistently delivering quality service.

Prescription

- **Promote the power of positive impressions**

A key part of the customer service delivery puzzle is the formation of the right image of the organization. As companies build their brand, they try to create a story about their company that can be used as the driver for interactions between them and their customers. Individual service providers also have the opportunity to create an individual brand which works in tandem with the broader corporate splash. If this does not occur, the experience could tend to be characterized by boring and robotic activities. There is therefore the opportunity for managers to promote to their teams the power of creating an individual service brand which complements what their company represents. In this case, Lucy did that without being in conflict with, or detracting from, what the overall corporate goals were. She did nothing illicit or outside of the company policy, but at the same time she distinguished herself from her peers. It did not mean her peers were doing poorly at their tasks.

In a real simple way, all she did was find a way to express the fact that she cared about her customers and would do a few things more, to ensure that they felt it worthwhile to shop at that particular grocery store. The value she offered to her company could be multiplied exponentially if the same mentality and actions were demonstrated by others. This by no means suggests the formation of some cheesy, marketing program to create corporate brand awareness. It is a recommendation to promote the "brand" of the individual service provider. The person can remain a unique, critical part of the service delivery team, while at the same time espousing a personal brand that captivates and speaks to the importance of making customers feel special.

Chapter 13 – Customers have choices

Like everyone who takes out a mortgage, who feels the pain of being saddled with an important debt for half one's lifetime, I was trying to find ways to reduce the stress that came with it. We had secured our mortgage while we were barely credit worthy and had progressed steadily to where we were comfortably managing the payments and securing other things of value. At one point, as interest rates declined, I started thinking that there had to be a better way of dealing with the persistent interest charges and the cloud of limited progress that was always hanging over my head, at least, that is how it felt. As the end of the initial three year term on my mortgage approached, I started exploring options. Luckily, near the same time I was introduced to a company that assisted families in managing their finances and restructuring debt. After a few meetings, I capitalized on the opportunity to have a consultation. While I was not a certified financial planner, or anything similar, I was by no means naive to the workings of capital. My work experience included a stint with a financial regulator which allowed me close proximity to many discussions on corporate and personal financial matters. In going into the consultation I was clear on some of the outcomes I wanted, the greatest of which was an alternative to the dreaded feeling I got from having a mortgage.

Our meeting went well and many ideas were presented

on how we could approach the refinancing of our debt. After some simple number crunching, the financial advisor showed us some options which would have resulted in savings, even if relatively nominal. While he was not the provider or approver of the new debt structure, he provided us a contact at a bank with which we had done some business before. He explained that his organization always made referrals to institutions and from those referrals they made a commission. While the model was somewhat new to us, our quest for financial freedom and less stress made it an attractive proposition. We called the contact at the bank, a lady named Doreen who was the most pleasant person you could meet. Our appointment was easily arranged and while the branch was at a polar opposite end of the city, the likely outcome quickly offset the distance.

Our initial meeting went well. There was a lot of paperwork required to start the process and it also required a second visit, maybe a third, to the branch to meet with Doreen. She took all our information, outlined the optional items associated with the debt model that we had selected and advised that there was an approval process that would take a short time. She spent most of her time getting to know us as customers and zoning in on the financial needs which led us to her. There was no reading of all the limitations to the model, or the similarity of products offered by other banks. Our meeting lasted nearly two hours at the end of which we felt there was hope of cutting nearly ten years off our initial mortgage while also providing some degree of financial freedom at the same time. The model appeared attractive especially the offering of an interest rate equal to the prime rate. For rookies in a country of many options, we felt like we were being offered a deal that would have normally been reserved for others that were wealthier and more financially savvy.

After leaving Doreen's office, my wife and I chatted about the meeting and the warmth that Doreen exuded. Not only was she knowledgeable but also personable. She was very experienced at what she did and brought all of that pedigree to bear on our experience with her. There were a few items that had to be completed prior to our next meeting, including a termination of the transaction with our current mortgagor and a transition of the debt to the new institution. While I had all but accepted the new debt structure that was crafted by Doreen, I wanted to explore the options that my current bank would have been willing to provide. I had no reason for deep loyalty to them but considered it proper to offer them the right to first refusal for my business. Yes, I was only a small, relatively insignificant borrower but I thought my business was important. I made an appointment to visit the bank to discuss my options.

The meeting with the representative was quick and very pointed. She outlined a few options that were available to me and pointed me to a promotion that was being offered to all customers that I could benefit from. The offer was nothing special. I had seen it before and was not interested. I asked her why they had not proactively contacted me to offer me a better rate especially since my mortgage term was about to expire? She explained that it was not their practice to do that as customers could search for offers on their own. I then advised her that I was in the process of transferring my business to another institution and required some documentation to complete the transfer. She quickly advised me that I should be careful of the attractiveness of the offer as it was not uncommon for customers to retrace their steps because that bank had not lived up to its promise. I was shocked at the advice presented and questioned the strategy being employed. The attempt to create doubt in my mind regarding the services of the competitor did not provide any additional confidence in their willingness to treat me in a special way. Instead, it removed my lingering thoughts of staying with that organization. All my wavering disappeared; my business had to move.

Within a few days all the requirements to establish my new line of credit, transfer existing loans and open the required accounts were completed. The new debt regime kicked in and we were able to start enjoying a new feeling regarding our debt. We were never extravagant spenders and were therefore not worried about the potential negative impacts of more disposable income. In fact, the extra dollars that we identified went into other savings instruments. There were a few loose ends to complete after our second meeting with Doreen and she promised to get them all sorted out and call us thereafter to provide an update. She did as she promised and wished us all the best in our financial management. A painless restructuring of our debt had occurred in the smoothest of ways. In the process there was the opportunity to notice business differentiators in action. I still could not understand the approach taken by my original bank regarding my mortgage. I was in the market for renewal options and nothing was offered but for a negative perspective on a competitor. While that was being done, the competitor was making an unchallenged offer for my business. What choice did I have but to gobble up what the competitor was presenting. Once we read the critical fine prints, we signed on the dotted line.

The value of options cannot be overstated especially in

areas regarding financial matters. While I have no scientific study to support my theory, I am convinced that the significant majority of people, who are provided options which made them better financially, would readily choose what was most beneficial. I am also of the view that when faced with options, a customer is likely to choose a path where benefit is optimized while effort is at a minimum. In this case, if a reasonable offer was made by my current bank, I would not have been inclined to make a change. I had no allegiance to Doreen or her bank, which meant there was a window for a successful counter offer by my current bank. As a customer, I was also open to finding a solution that met, or went closest, to my needs. Most of the big banks had similar products. The extent to which they offered those products to ordinary customers like me, was often built on discretion. The agent had the option, in my view, to make me an offer which was better than the standard promotion and she chose not to. I had the opportunity to choose between the incumbent mortgagor and a new one and I exercised my option to choose.

We have not changed banks since. Our financial situation has improved as our careers progressed and we have remained loyal while searching for options to earn better returns on our investments. There have been many positive experiences with this new institution which have solidified the reputation of the organization in our minds. I would purport that they understand that customers have options and may decide to move their business to other institutions. Often the decision is based on the service quality comparison versus a product comparison especially in a marketplace where pseudo oligopolies abound with limited differentiation.

Prescription

- **Don't take the customers right to choose for granted**

It is not uncommon for an organization's success to become its Achilles heel. This happens because the recognition of what led to their success in the first place is lost. It is not uncommon for some degree of arrogance and ambivalence to become part of the cultural fabric which leads to a devaluation of the importance of the common customers. In many of these situations, the best service options, perks and products are reserved for the high-spending customer only. The regular customer who previously was the foundation on which the organization was built loses status. Consequently, service levels to this category of customer falls.

In the experience with my bank, I would argue that had I been a multi-millionaire with a large portfolio, the approach to me would have been starkly different, which it should. That said, the baseline service should never have been set that low. To remedy the likelihood of this happening, I would recommend that organizations establish baseline service levels which do not devalue the importance of those at the lower end of the customer value continuum. In doing this, there is the opportunity to capitalize on business from all ends of the spectrum. As is generally the case, the majority of the customers will fit in an "average" category. This does not mean their value should be ignored.

No business wants to see customers walk away. In the end however, the customers have the power to choose. This should not be taken for granted. In providing service, those managing the execution of strategy should ensure that teams are conscious of, and prepared to deal with the impact of this important factor. Recognizing this, and developing appropriate responses, could create wins for both customers and the organization.

Chapter 14 – Colleagues are customers too

I was in the midst of implementing a development program for potential leaders in my team. It was a new program aimed at bridging our succession gap. One module of the program was a session on "Managing Conflict". I approached a manager in our human resources team to develop and present the session. She recommended another manager in her team as she was busy on other projects. I took the time to meet with the manager and explain my requirements. At the end of the discussion she asked that I send her an email formalizing my request while outlining the details. I did that the next day. This was to ensure that I was well placed in her queue of projects. I appreciated that everyone had different priorities.

Two months went by without a response from the manager. The silence forced me to conclude that it had fallen off her radar. Instead of waiting on her, I arranged to have another person present the topic to support the program. I tried to ensure that there was continuity in the program and had numerous options in the event, as in this case, the first choice presenter failed to deliver. The substitute presentation went very well with positive feedback from the participants. Another session in the program was complete and I moved on to the next.

The question of the status of my request continued to linger in my mind. I was torn between ignoring the silence

wondered how she had treated other peers. It led me to think that she was not the only one in our organization who got too busy, or was just negligent, to acknowledge the feelings of their peers. It begged the question of whether the quality of service meted to peers was similar to that meted to customers. I hoped that was not the case as it would have reflected poorly on both the individual and the organization. If the poor treatment was only directed to peers, then it meant there was a coaching opportunity. It still however triggered a consciousness in me regarding how I looked at the treatment I got from my colleagues. I always had standards regarding my responsiveness to requests, irrespective of the sources. My line of work forced me to be focussed on the need of customers. To that extent, being responsive was a key component of my professional DNA. I therefore, behaved that way to everyone.

Often it is forgotten that at the end of each request are real customer needs that are merely being served by an intermediary. Our program was geared at building the skills of our customer service agents to enable them to interact in a more comprehensive, yet comfortable, way with our customers. The training provided was expected to positively impact customer experiences. I doubt that my request was looked at that way. I recalled that sometime the same year, I had the opportunity to speak to a team in our manufacturing department. They were primarily responsible for procuring and making some of our products. In the discussion with them, I explained the concept of the multiplier effect that different teams had to consider when delivering service. I explained that when we sold to a reseller, the experience is multiplied several hundred times as he then sells to hundreds of customers who either relish or despise the product they purchased. The downstream effect of the contribution made by the manufacturing team does not end with a transaction to the reseller but passes many times over to customers and potential customers. It was critical therefore that everyone assessed their value and take steps to ensure that it is optimal in all processes.

While it seems unlikely, all processes have the potential of affecting how a customer feels. All contributors to these processes should understand that, and contribute accordingly. Within an organization, it is critical to establish the concept, and ensure understanding, of the value chain. There should also be standards to drive the desired output. Most importantly, is the appreciation that all efforts within the myriad of processes are geared at having customers feel good about working with, and purchasing the goods and services created within those processes. Anything otherwise would be counter productive.

Prescription

- **Service delivery is a value chain everyone should understand**

There is the likelihood that a distinction in service quality exists in most organizations where external customers are given a higher level of service. While in some instances there is merit to this, as tiered service levels are not uncommon, it is important to ensure that the gap between both is not detrimental to the overall quality of service. There also needs to be an appreciation of the service delivery value chain to ensure that an understanding exists about the correlation between internal service delivery and external customer satisfaction. Organizations should therefore attempt to install processes and set values which allow for an effective translation of internal service standards to the overall customer experience. There is a value chain that needs to be understood, if not, the perception of the impact of service delivery would be limited to simple functional processes and no connection to the end customer is created. It is recommended that in all programs aimed at developing customer service skills, a clear correlation be made between what appears to be obscure back-office processes and the ultimate customer experience. In fact, many of the things that happen in the back-office will have some effect on how the customer ultimately feels.

It is also recommended that all staff training programs focus on the concept of the internal customer relationships. In this process, the individuals would be able to identify their impact on the different customer interactions. With this appreciation, the correlation of internal customer standards with the external customer expectations would be more easily aligned. In the end, when the right habits are developed, whether the customer was internal or external would become moot as the service quality would be unchanged.

Chapter 15 – "I am closed for the day"

It was near Christmas and I needed to get a haircut. I knew there would be a line-up at my regular barber who operated on a first come, first serve basis. I arrived there about an hour before closing time and from the many cars in the parking lot I knew I was in for a long wait. This was a very popular barber shop within the community which was known for the cultural mix and camaraderie. While the wait was sometimes frustrating, the quality of the haircut and the understanding of the barbers of the styles required by the customers, made the wait rewarding on most occasions. I had been going to this barber shop for near three years, and considered myself a regular customer that was known by the owner and the staff. On previous visits we had many interesting conversations on a range of topics although they always seemed to evolve to end with a discussion on sports.

There was a large number of customers waiting as I entered the shop. All available seats were taken. As was customary when the place was crowded, I moved to add my name to the waiting list when the owner, Ted, curtly said, "no more names, we are closed". I smiled and responded that there was still an hour to closing time based on the hours of operation listed on the door. He replied that it did not matter what the sign said, they were not taking any more customers for the day. I understood that their day would extend way past the normal operating hours because of the number of customers there. I could not understand the curt, unsociable response. I stood there for a minute feeling hurt and embarrassed. I could not believe that I was being treated that way. I turned and left and he walked behind me and locked the door. I concluded that he was not prepared to say the same thing again and closing the door would have eliminated that need.

I drove home angered by the occurrence and saddened that someone, whom I had always respected, did not think it proper to extend a reasonable dose of respect to me. I wondered if he had behaved the same way to other customers prior to my getting there. I thought that maybe he was just "having a bad day" and acted out of character with me. A range of thoughts filled my mind as I replayed the encounter numerous times on my way home. With each replay, I found I could not accept the behaviour as reasonable. There was no need to be rude to me. It was not something that I was going to easily forget. I had also started thinking of the options available to me.

In the past, I had supported his business faithfully and despite the extended wait times, was never actively seeking an alternative provider for the services that were offered. A haircut, while important, was by no means an overly technical task and I knew if I took the time, I would have found someone equally capable of providing me with a satisfactory experience. The manner in which he spoke to me triggered my search. As I drove, I decided that I would never use Ted's services again. I preferred to risk the potential ridicule of a horrible haircut or spend more to get it done. Finding a new barber was now important to making me feel better.

A few weeks later, after making a few phone calls, I was introduced to another barber, Christian. He was someone I was acquainted with but I was not aware that he was a barber. I also knew the operator of the salon but was never keen to go there because of the clientele that he catered to. It was a contrasting setting to what I had been accustomed. I now needed to make an appointment, be on time and engage in discussions that were more unisex which was in line with the offerings of this shop; it catered to hair needs for both genders. For the first few appointments it felt a bit uncomfortable as it was never easy to engage for any extended period in the limited conversations that occurred. I got past that quickly and enjoyed the change of scenery and the civility that I encountered every time I went there. It did cost me a little more, however, the comfort of the setting and the time savings were worth each extra dollar. Each visit reinforced the lower standard that I had been subscribing loyally to for many years with no justifiable reason. I also felt that my business would not be missed. It was unlikely that it would have any noticeable effect on Ted's bottom line. With all that, what was it that kept me going there? There was no overriding reason to have been a loyal customer besides the fact that there were no compelling reasons to change. Yes, I had often wanted to save time but it did not make me feel unwanted, or disrespected, to wait my turn when I went there. The rates he charged were reasonable; cost was therefore not an issue. Like most humans, no change was needed when nothing was broken. Yes, there could have been better processes however the base service was tolerable.

I never related the story to anyone. I did not feel like doing that. I knew many persons who were customers of Ted's, however, I did not feel driven to share my encounter with them. I figured that they would have had their own reasons for continuing to use his services. While there are many persons who would have likely placed the incident on the community headlines, which would have possibly led to some fallout, I figured that the market was such that there were others who would have forgiven and forgotten the incident. I did not, at least the part about forgetting.

For the next two years, I enjoyed the positive treatment I got at my new barber. The feeling was worth the change and extra cost. He was present for every appointment and I was never asked to wait beyond reason. In addition to that, he was always very pleasant and engaging. I always felt valued and respected there. Due to some new regulatory requirements, Christian had to terminate his work with the salon. Interestingly, I never even considered going back to Ted. Luckily I found a new option which was even more convenient and also satisfied my need to feel good about the service being offered to me.

Prescription

- **Make all communication respectful**

Every business will encounter abnormal circumstances where the desired service level to customers is not met. In most cases, reasonable customers will understand the challenge and respond in an acceptable matter. The customers' patience may be tested if the service level continues to deteriorate with no sign of improvement. If within the same context, there are expressions, whether intended or incidental, which display arrogance, apathy or disregard for the customer, the situation could turn sour really quickly. All customers, however relatively insignificant their value to the overall success of a business, deserve to be treated with respect. This should be reflected in all communications from the organization. Additionally, all subsequent messaging should reflect an appreciation for the customers' patience during the times of below par service levels.

Ted and his team would be best advised to create a simple, respectful message next time they are unable to satisfy customer demand. A note on the door or a pleasant message would have been sufficient for the situation. While disappointed, I am sure the negative emotions that occurred would have been spared had the approach been different. Larger organizations could also learn from this as the impersonality of some messages lead to similar feelings. Customers feel almost dehumanized by the approach and thereafter consider themselves statistics as opposed to a special person contributing to an organization's growth and success.

Customers place value on their loyalty to an organization. Businesses do the same thing. For many businesses, "goodwill" is a tremendous asset. Investment is made to maintain that value. If the actions taken by these businesses are seen as abrasive and offensive, the value of that goodwill can eroded. This undermines the effort made to develop that value. In the case of Ted's business, the goodwill that was built over several years, evaporated within minutes. In fact, one sentence was all it took.

Chapter 16 – Self correction is great

I was in a Marriott hotel in Oakland, California for a conference in San Francisco. My travel agent was unable to secure a room within walking distance of the convention centre. The thought of having to commute daily to the event did not excite me and the description some colleagues gave me of the city did not inspire any sense of pleasure. The hotel was under renovation, and, fortunately, I was allocated a room on the recently renovated 9th floor, as described by the lady at the check-in counter. As was typical for me after a day of delayed flights, I headed to my room, dropped my bag and quickly found the hotel restaurant. Due to the renovations at the hotel, access to the restaurant was not as straightforward but having gotten there, I seated myself and watched the latest sports news while I waited to be served. Soon I was brought a menu and offered something to drink. My choice of entrée was soon delivered and I thoroughly enjoyed my meal, paid and retired to my room to prepare for the next day.

After a long day at the conference, where it felt like I had walked a thousand miles, I returned to my hotel room, worked on some emails and then hit the fitness centre for a quick round of cardio. Like always happens at conferences, the networking sometimes lead to over-consumption of calories in the wrong food groups. For this conference, I was conscious to avoid that, and promised to stick to a regimented eating and fitness routine. After the gym and a quick shower I headed to the restaurant.

Earlier, the clerk at the front desk had provided me with a list of nearby restaurants and even highly recommended a few. I thought about exploring the area but concluded that the service at the hotel restaurant, City Limits Grill, had been so good the night before that I deferred the option to explore and stayed within the confines of the hotel. On arrival, I chose to seat myself as I had done the night. A few other customers arrived after I did and they chose to be seated by the host who offered them menus and drinks. I was not. I realized that I had not been seated which may have led the rather busy hosts to assume that I was already greeted and served. I was not bothered in the least as I had time and was really only interested in getting a soup and salad before going back to my room.

About ten minutes had passed when I finally signalled to the host and asked for a menu. Very soon a server, James, arrived and took my order. I had noticed James moving briskly between tables addressing the different customer needs. While the restaurant was not packed, there was a steady flow of customers to consume the time of all the staff. I had overheard him saying that another colleague had gone on break and he was covering for her. That explained why I had been there unnoticed for so long. On returning with my appetizer James apologized profusely for the extended wait time. He pleasantly advised that to compensate for my extended wait, all, but my salad, would be free. For the next thirty minutes, he checked with me on a regular basis. At the point of bringing the check, he apologized again, reminded me of the reduced charges and complimented me on being a great guest. As he had stated, all I paid for was my salad. I did however tip him generously for all that he gave me for free. In my mind the service was great and did not require the apologies and concessions that he made. What stood out was his acknowledgement that the service was below par, which he was keen to remediate quickly.

I left the restaurant wondering how many customers would be encouraged offer more business to an organization if there was a policy which required staff to correct perceived inadequacies in a proactive way. In this case, he made me feel way more important than I needed to as the oversight was not a major offence to me. James would have also been conscious that hotels were temporary homes for transient guests and that resolution had to be immediate. Even though the concession that he made was immaterial from a financial perspective, it was significant to know that he was so willing to make an offer which no one would refuse.

For the week that I stayed in the city, I ate at the restaurant at least once daily. James had ensured more revenue for the City Limits Grill by his proactive, professional approach. As a customer, there is always that special feeling when that level of service is received. It was no different for me. Thereafter, each time I went there, I made a conscious effort to see how the staff treated guests. As expected, there was always a constant effort to provide fast, pleasant service. On a few occasions I saw James, who was delivering the same high quality service that he delivered to me. I was not surprised that the restaurant was always busy and I am sure there were other customers that were satisfied, maybe even impressed, with the work that James and the other members of staff did to make them feel important.

Prescription

- **Proactive resolutions create a winning opportunity**

The training manual for many customer focused teams is often based on actions and activities that are responses to customers' expressed needs. This is generally accepted as necessary to maintain common standards and have consistent customer experiences. It is also crucial that in designing these programs, consideration be given to the need, and value, of having components which train employees in being proactive. This proactivity includes the ability to quickly identify potential dissatisfiers and proposing, or implementing, a solution to correct the situation. While it creates a counterpoint to the generally accepted reactive mentality in a customer service environment, it provides an opportunity to transform the customer experience which not only recovers the goodwill that may have been marginally affected, but sets the organization apart as forward thinking and deserving of future business.

All organizations should ensure that employees are allowed the opportunity to exercise reasonable judgement in resolving issues that they consider to be threats to the image, and financial success, of the organization. There should also be methods to periodically reinforce this. Reinforcement for the reactive components is a standard part of most operations. The elite organizations will also dedicate some time to focussing on the proactive components to ensure that all staff maintain the understanding of how important that component is to creating a competitive advantage for the organization.

Chapter 17 – Service from the captain

I was off to another conference. While I was comfortable flying, I was always aware of the inherent risk in getting into an aircraft. A few years back I was fortunate to enjoy an experience in a flight simulator. Since then my respect for the work done by pilots increased significantly. For this conference, I was travelling on a Sunday on a United Airlines flight into California. I was never fond of United because their planes were old, noisy and had no entertainment system. To our city, they always flew regional jets which had really limited leg room to compound their already basic transportation offering.

The boarding process moved quickly and soon the aircraft was almost completely full. A young couple were last to board the plane. The lady took the seat beside me while her partner sat across the aisle. From the conversation with her partner, I learned that they had been travelling from Europe and after nearly twenty-four hours on airplanes, you could sense she was somewhat frustrated. I am sure moving from a large trans-Atlantic jet to a regional jet was not most desirable. As the cabin crew made final preparations for departure, the stewardess approached the male passenger and curtly advised him that in preparation for departure he needed to stow his bag or pass it to the front to be tagged and stored in the baggage compartment. He did not respond to her. You could sense the flames that engulfed their emotions as the stewardess walked away.

The irony of the situation was that the passenger was aware that his bag would not have fit in the overhead compartment and was taking out some valuables and fragile items, as advised by the agent at the boarding gate, prior to having it tagged for storage in cargo hold. They were a few minutes late from their connecting flight, and with the understanding of the gate agent, he agreed to quickly get it done while onboard. He was in the process of doing this when the stewardess made her statement. Neither passenger responded, which said a lot, and as the stewardess walked away the lady commented on how unhelpful she was to go with her rude attitude. She recalled all the notable events of their last day to highlight how the last thirty seconds had impacted it. I don't think the stewardess heard her, or if she did, she acted as if she didn't. For a few minutes the gentleman rummaged through his bag taking out items. He was about to close his bag when the captain, who was greeting passengers as they entered the aircraft, came by. He said that the flight was almost ready to go and offered to assist the passenger with his bag. The passenger took a few more valuables from his bag and then passed it to the captain who had waited patiently on him. The captain took his bag to the jetway, had it tagged and stored and returned with a baggage ticket for the passenger. By now, the lady was commenting on the contrasting behaviour of the two crew members. I was impressed with the attitude of the captain.

As an onlooker to the situation, there were many things that jumped at me from a customer service perspective. None of the participants had any reason to look at it the way I did. They were active players. The passengers had emotional baggage that made their nerves understandably sensitive. Airline travel does that to some people. The stewardess was merely doing her job and was not catering to what their day had been like to that point. Reasonably, can someone in that role cater to all the emotional possibilities passengers may be facing? Maybe not! The captain, while doing the same as the stewardess, offered a helping hand. That was the only difference. Yet, the significance of that action could be felt by those who were actively involved as well as those who merely paid interest to what occurred.

As the door to the aircraft closed and the plane began the push back from the gate, the captain advised that there would be a delayed departure due to weather conditions at our destination and traffic adjustments made by air traffic control. I anticipated a negative reaction from the lady. After all they had endured to that point, another delay would surely add salt to their wounds. To my surprise, she remained calm and positioned herself to have a nap. Who could have anticipated such a response considering her agitation earlier? There was no doubt that the interaction with the captain a few minutes earlier had placed her in a better mood to deal with the news.

The captain spoke to the passengers for what I considered an extended time explaining the situation and the steps that would be taken to have us airborne in the shortest possible time. Twice in an hour I was impressed by the captain's efforts. It was clear that the captain understood and acted in response to how customers are likely to feel. It was also good to see that he appreciated that customers would be more appreciative if they saw him as someone who cared. Often in the travel industry, pilots are noted only for the stress, complexity and risk associated with their roles. However, here was a circumstance where this pilot was actively involved in delivering service, and creating positive feelings in customers, as a part of his role.

We arrived in California after a smooth, uneventful flight. On arrival we were advised of a further delay, as, due to our late arrival, there was no gate available. Once again the captain exhibited his well developed people skills to explain the situation and ask for continued patience. As a customer, what would otherwise be a source of negative emotions, was only a slight inconvenience. The captain had been such an awesome customer service agent, that the message was positively received, in fact, there was more sympathy for the captain and crew than anything else. The lady beside me read for almost all the time we sat on the tarmac waiting for a gate to become available. She too, I concluded, had been effectively treated by the captain, which led to her being as calm as she was. Imagine if the stewardess had made the announcement, which although highly unlikely was also a possibility. In response, not only was it likely that they would have remembered the incident at the start of the flight but they may also have been tempted to respond sarcastically or in some other way which reflected their negative feelings.

As the leader of the crew on that United Airlines flight, the captain exhibited leadership in many different ways. His management of the situation with the delay was exemplary, as was his willingness to assist the male passenger with his bag. In both circumstances, there may have been other approaches which would not have reflected the customer care and leadership. He did not rely only on his team to be the face to the customer. He was an active participant in the process and made a positive contribution to negate the sub-par performance of another member of his team.

Prescription

- **Delivering quality service comes from all levels**

It is not uncommon within an organization to see senior managers disassociate themselves from the core operating principles applied at the individual contributor levels. Depending on the culture of the organization, it could be construed as normal. In such situations, there are double standards which often create mental rifts. While there needs to be an acceptance of the roles and responsibilities at the different levels within an organization, there is significant value in having core principles apply to all within the organization, especially when it comes to treating the customer correctly. In the experience with the pilot, it was clear that he did not think he was beyond providing basic customer service to passengers on his flight. It was a part of his role, wherever required, to ensure not only the safety of passengers, but also to contribute positively to the way they felt about purchasing a seat with the airline that employed him.

It is good practice, and recommended for all organizations, to instil and recognize that quality service has inputs from all levels. Leading by example has the potential to generate positive energy in organizations and provide the impetus for consistently excellent service. The leadership provided within an organization will ultimately reflect on the quality of the service experience. Quality service from all levels contributes significantly to a quality culture.

Chapter 18 – Value-added hair service

In chapter 15, I recalled my experience with a barber and how it led to my decision to find someone else to provide that service. Christian, my new barber, was forced to terminate his business. I was in the market again. How I found a new barber was somewhat bizarre.

I was asked to deliver an item to a salon operated by a member of my community association. While there, I asked if they catered to male customers to which they said yes. With that, for the first time, I opted to have a female attend to my hair needs. I needed the service and I was open to the risk. There was a tinge of fear that it could have been a devastating experience however, I had all the damage control elements at the ready. Dionne, the hairdresser, was someone I had known, but never imagined one day sitting in her chair with the buzzing sound of shears in the background. After a few visits, and some suggestions on how to get the cut nearer to what I wanted, my comfort level continued to grow. I loved the fact that her salon was only five minutes from my office and also on the route to my home. The convenience was priceless. I could make a same day appointment and have my hair cut on the way home.

The first six months were absolutely fantastic and the look and feel that came with each visit improved. I felt relaxed, satisfactorily groomed and pleased that I had finally found a solution, which despite opportunities for improvement, met my needs and left me with a good feeling after each visit. Dionne and I developed an excellent rapport and she started giving me tips on how to take care of my hair. Like most of the men I knew, going to a stylist was a simple occurrence with a single-minded expectation; a haircut that did not make you look like a weirdo. I had arranged a schedule with her of being there every three to four weeks as, with my increasing family of grey hair, I wanted to maintain a consistent low cut to limit their immediate attention. This was working great until I called to make an appointment and found out she was on vacation. The person answering, Elsie, was the owner of the salon and someone I knew fairly well. She advised me that Dionne would be away for two weeks but I could set my appointment as normal. I figured that since Dionne was away that I would benefit from Elsie's experience. When I arrived I was ushered to a chair manned by Jamelia. Here I was having a seat in her chair and getting ready for a new experience. I said to her what I had always said to Dionne, take it low and don't get bothered about styling. Off she went.

She trimmed, combed and clipped for about twenty minutes then asked me to have a look. I told her it looked fine and she did some finishing touches and began removing the covering cloth used to protect customers' clothes. I was ready to leave when she pointed me to the sink. She was going to wash out the remaining hair cuttings before I left. In all the years that I had been to barber shops, and even while Dionne did my hair, it had never been suggested that a quick wash could be done to complete the process. It was awesome! Not only was the feeling of the warm rush from the tap rejuvenating, the thought that a task that took an additional ten minutes could have been so satisfying was mind-blowing. Why did

Jamelia think of this when no one before ever thought of it? I was tempted to ask if this was something special that she thought of because it was the first time I was her customer. I did not. I wallowed in the feeling and tipped her nicely on my way out. All the way home, I thought to myself that it was such a wonderful feeling and worth every dollar and minute I had spent there. There was nothing special about the haircut, in fact, on second review, it could have been better. However the experience I left with outdid all the others that I had ever had.

A few weeks later I had a business trip and wanted to freshen up before taking off for a week of meetings with executives of other companies. I called and booked a haircut. Dionne had taken an extended vacation which led to another appointment with Jamelia. It was a day when they weren't overly busy, which allowed me a spot in the prime hours of the afternoon. Once there, I told her of the areas that could have improved from the last time which she readily understood. Another twenty minutes of trimming, combing and clipping passed. She had me look and confirm if it was done as I desired. It was fine with me. Once again, she directed me to the sink for a quick rinse. Once again, I wallowed in the aura of the feeling. While there was a physical component to what I was enjoying, I was captured more by the internal warmth it created for me as a customer. I told Elsie on my way out that Jamelia had created a customer for life as through an experience which was unlikely to be matched by anyone else. Not for a moment was I suggesting that Dionne did not provide great service. Jamelia had introduced a value added component, which did not cost me anything more, which was hard to outdo.

With each visit thereafter, I received the same treatment. When Dionne returned, it became the norm. Even after ten visits, the new service level did not lose the value added feel. It got me thinking of the many circumstances which were created everyday where customers are provided with a value added component to the service that they purchased. It is also true that the opportunity is allowed to go to waste as well, and customers leave with the standard, "out-of-the-box" service experience. A customer receiving the standard service would have no reason to complain as their basic requirements are being met, pleasantly and professionally. However, the customers receiving the value-added components can attest to the greater level of satisfaction that is derived and the increased sense of loyalty that automatically develops. In the case of my hair salon, the cost for the additional component was negligible. It took a few extra minutes, ounces of product and a few gallons of water. The impact on me was way greater than the value of those items. The goodwill that Jamelia created by adding a quick rinse to an otherwise mundane haircut experience, could not be immediately quantified. Should at some point Elsie choose to sell that business, this build-up of loyalty added value to her sale price and provided negotiating power. Many businesses have benefited greatly from value-added service because it creates goodwill and makes customers have a good feeling.

Prescription

- **Plan to exceed customer expectations**

Most customers accept standard service as reasonable. It meets basic needs and reflects an agreement on the value that was presented for the good or service being consumed. Even with that understanding, it is also true that all customers appreciate service that exceeds the value displayed and the expectation that they had. With that in mind, it is useful for organizations to consider exploiting the significant potential of a strategy of a value-added component, as part of what is perceived as basic service. The key is to create differentiation without necessarily changing the organizations investment requirement. If this can be achieved, there are huge returns to be derived, and in many cases, sustainable value through goodwill and other real assets. For example, some customers are prepared to pay premium prices for experiences where value added features are likely to be presented. This leads to greater product margins and repeat business. In other cases, the rate of referral increases as a function of the impact of the value-added services offered. No matter what the circumstance, there are winning elements to having a value added strategy. Just think, if you can add some sparkle to a reasonably satisfying experience, how is the customer likely to feel and what are the returns for the organization?

I would recommend that organizations keen on creating differentiation find ways to add to the pleasure of customer experiences. By employing a strategy aimed at beating customer expectations consistently, there is the potential for increased loyalty and increased revenue. Employees should therefore be empowered, and encouraged, to contribute to this strategy. Customers are always left with positive feelings whenever their expectations are exceeded and, in many cases, are prepared to invest more into such organizations. Making a customer feel "even better", provides positive returns.

Chapter 19 – Why should the customer wait?

Many of the events mentioned in this book happened in businesses that I was not related to. I was the customer or an observer of a customer experience that resonated with me. As I may have mentioned a few times, I have spent over a decade leading customer service organizations. There are likely many stories like the ones captured here that our customers could write regarding the experiences they have had with members of my team. As I worked on this project, I began taking time to observe in greater detail some of the happenings within my own domain. I figured it would be fair to turn the spotlight on what I had been doing to build a world class team, which delivered consistently above our customers' expectations. I discovered that while we did well, there were many opportunities for improvement. The episode below captures that.

It was October and our global channel meetings were being held. It was usually an intense four days of meetings and discussions on performance, forecast and issues. Being in the services team meant I spent the greater part of those days on the performance and issues components. While for some it was challenging and energy sapping, we enjoyed the task of addressing the tough issues that faced our customers. In many cases, we were already working on resolutions and in others we were just happy to get feedback. In one of the meetings, a partner principal raised the issue of less than acceptable response times from my teams. I was a little surprised at the examples being provided and asked for some additional information to facilitate my investigation of what had transpired. Once back in the office, I went to the team in question to try to understand what had occurred. The responses were interesting.

Both persons that were involved in the case mentioned by the customer were quickly able to provide me with a summary of what had happened. The timeline was similar to that provided by the customer however the perspective was very different. The case in particular related to the customer's request for a set of replacement parts for a defective product. The product was under warranty. The customer suggested that we provide an additional buffer stock as it was likely that there would be other failures which would require repair. As an organization, the decision to provide additional parts for that product had already been made. Unfortunately, at that time there was very little inventory of the parts which meant there were delays in fulfilling standard orders for the product. The fact that the customer was requesting additional product created a decision point which became the "issue". After five days of waiting for a resolution, the customer was agitated at the service level from my team. He had not been provided with a decision on his request, which was compounded by the fact that no product had shown up at his store. I asked my team why the customer had not been advised of what was going to be done. They advised me that they were waiting on an update on inventory in order to make the decision. It was a little illogical to me so I drilled a little deeper into what had been done.

A request had been made for an update on inventory which had not been promptly responded to. Not wanting to provide an answer which did not include the precise number of products to be sent to the customer, my team continued to wait on the response from our logistics team. While this waiting occurred, the customer was left waiting as well. The conclusion had been made that an answer without the detail of the product quantity would have been below expectation. As I listened, I realized how much we had missed a very basic requirement in dealing with the customer issue. We failed to communicate the status of the resolution. In an effort to provide the best solution, we allowed a silent period to occur which made the customer feel that we did not take his request seriously. The feeling he had was that we did not want to acknowledge the issue he had raised and were busy trying to prove him wrong. Clearly the range of negative feelings widened with each day that passed.

After having the conversation with my team, it was important that I got back to the customer. It was a little embarrassing that my own team handled that issue the way they did. Having been in situations like that before, I also understood how he felt which made it a little easier to respond and provide a path to resolution. It also reinforced to me how crucial it was to constantly reinforce the focus and vision of our team. Often, even with the best intentions, the teams we manage lose focus of what is crucial. In many instances, the attempt to be perfect is thwarted by the realities that exist.

We resolved the issue the next day. Once resolved, I asked that immediate contact be made with the customer to provide an update and apology. From the lesson learned, I resolved to spend more time with my teams reinforcing the vision of our organization. Reinforcing the basics was an important part of recovering and growing into a world class support organization.

Prescription

- **Never stop reinforcing the basics**

The underachievement of my team, in this specific case, was humbling. Getting customer feedback was important to provide a test of the reality that existed for our customers. While not always an easy thing to accept, there will be situations which require in-depth analysis of the processes being employed in the delivery of service. The persons involved in the case above were experienced members of my team who remained in my confidence. That said, it was clear that an opportunity existed to revisit some of the values which drove our team. The need for reinforcement of our core principles was clear. We became focussed on our own business strategies and ideas and forgot the tremendous value of the customer service basics.

As a manager, it was my task to ensure that the teams remained focussed on what was likely to provide most value to customer. If that did not occur, I was responsible to ensure that was corrected. It was also my responsibility to have measures in place to keep the teams focussed on the basics of the service that we delivered. While customer feedback was a crucial component to our operations, our process should not be a reactive operation. All managers should establish a reinforcement mechanism within their operations. This would ensure that the many factors which occupied the day-to-day activities were tempered by the periodic reality check. With this in place, there would be greater confidence and awareness of the consistency, and quality, of the delivery, of the team.

Chapter 20 – A day late

In the previous chapter I recalled an event within my own team where one of my team members vacillated around making a decision which led to the customer being frustrated. I understood both perspectives but learnt from the episode that it is critical to ensure that the needs of the customer are understood and addressed, even if the complete solution was not available. At about the same time, I got an escalated email from one of our sales managers. There was an urgent, by his standards, customer issue that required immediate attention and he wanted me to appoint someone to resolve the issue. Part of his email included a chain of emails between the customer, a sales agent in the region and a channel partner. The tone of the email suggested that the sales manager had some remediation to do with the customer and the speedy resolution of the current issue would go some way in making that easier. Acknowledging the severity of his tone, I assigned the matter to one of my senior technicians who had many years of experience in the role. He had recently been on a customer site to address several critical issues and seemed energized about his role. My view was that he would quickly resolve the issue, provide an update to the relevant parties and move on to the many other important tasks that needed to be attended to. In my mind, it was a simple issue to resolve. The kind you would not mind having all the time.

A few days passed and I did not receive an update from him.

I concluded that it had been resolved and he had forgotten to advise me. On the weekend, I received another email from the sales manager asking for my immediate intervention, including contacting the customer, as the issue had not been resolved speedily or satisfactorily. The chain of email exchanges had grown and the customer's tone reflected increasing agitation. I was shocked and disappointed as I could not understand why a matter of such relative simplicity was not attended to. All that was required was a request for replacement products with specific instructions to expedite the shipment. No real complexity. On getting the email, I promptly requested an update on the situation. I was advised that all was done, that there had been a delay, however the product was shipped and would have arrived at the customer's site the next day. I expressed my thanks for the update, my disappointment with the handling of the situation and my hope that contact had been made with the customer to provide an update and apology for the less than satisfactory service. At minimum, that is what I would have expected as a customer.

The fact that the issue had not been satisfactorily handled influenced my decision to contact the customer. It is always a bonus to have the management of an organization communicate with the customer, even if the gesture is a token one. In this case, I wanted to reassure the customer that our organization was committed to world class support and that the recent experience was an aberration that we would ensure was not repeated.

The conversation with Heather, the customer, was interesting. She expressed appreciation for my effort, reiterated her dissatisfaction with the service provided and suggested a few things that we could do as an organization to improve. She also explained that she did receive an update from the person that I had assigned. While she appreciated his effort to recover her confidence, she explained that she had been in contact with another agent in our support team who had provided more up-to-date information than she had recently received from the person I had assigned. In her own words, she was further ahead than e was. He was a day behind.

Later that day I spoke to his manager about the incident. There was no point being angry, even though I will admit to a lingering feeling of disappointment. He had let me down by providing below par service to the customer. It also forced me to question whether we had done enough to reinforce the key components of our mission as a service organization. We had not. I would not have been dealing with the situation had we done that effectively. In recapping the events, I made the decision to have a chat with him to get his perspective on what had happened and how it could have been handled more effectively. He explained that he had a number of issues to resolve and forgot to complete a few tasks on the issue. In his view, he had done all the "major" things, including advising the customer of what was going to be done to resolve the issue. He said that as far as getting all done, he had really only missed a day. That was true. He had only missed a day however, it was the day that the customer lost patience, made the call to someone else and got information and resolution. It is likely that the agent she spoke to merely added a few simple clicks to complete the process that had already been started. In the eyes of the customer, the new agent had done what had been previously eluding everyone else. He completed the transaction. In this case, she was provided with a tracking number for the shipment and an estimated date for receipt. For her, that was major progress.

It was a coaching opportunity and I seized it. My entire team needed to hear the message. During that week, I had several meetings with all my teams to review some very simple concepts related to service delivery. My message was to remind them of the significance of minority opinions when dealing with customers. Sometimes, the voices of the minority are more resounding than expected. I also reinforced the importance of each fraction of time in the customer's perception about our service quality. In this case, my agent was a day behind the customer. It was also important for me to reinforce the power of one. Each person within the team was valuable to our operation. The impact of one interaction on the overall perception of the team is often unfortunate; however there is a reality that has to be accepted. To consistently succeed, the team relied on the quality input of all members.

The customer received the replacement product, had it installed and was back to normal operations. That was important to our organization. The numerous negative feelings that were felt during the process were not desirable. It reinforced our need to continue working hard at delivering a world class customer experience, everytime.

Prescription

- **The customer's expectations are always rising**

There are many factors that provide increased power to the customer. Technology, competition, economic conditions and knowledge are a few which have tremendous impact in a dynamic market. There is therefore increased pressure on organizations to be constantly improving, while also creating winning differentiation. The laggards in these situations are squeezed out of business while those that pay most attention, and invest accordingly, stand out as beacons to be emulated.

A key component in the success equation is accepting that the standards are constantly being forced upwards and responding positively is a requirement to succeed. As reflected in the events above, the customer was impatient, discerning and willing to exercise options where possible. The agent may have assumed that his pace would have been acceptable to the customer. It was not. Even worse, the customer did not think it worthwhile to advise the agent that it was not. As happens so often, they move on while glancing back to see if you are aware of how far ahead they are. All organizations involved in the delivery of service must ensure that there are mechanisms to constantly measure the pulse of the market and the expectations of customers. Additionally, resolution time and customer satisfaction should be tracked and reinforced to constantly push teams to higher levels of performance. Anything less could spell ultimate disaster as the customer would have long moved ahead as other organizations in the market find ways to meet their constantly growing expectations.

Conclusion

This collection of experiences could go on *ad nauseum* but I will stop here. From all the interactions contained in these pages, there are numerous themes and conclusions that could be drawn. There are also numerous ways that the customer or the service delivery agent could have responded in all the situations. Whatever the changes that could have been applied to each scenario, there are some fundamentals that remain throughout, the most important being the need to recognize that the millions of interactions that occur as part of business transactions daily, impact how people feel, and by extension, their spending patterns, their referral to that organization and their repeat business.

Organizations, in acknowledging market and other economic challenges, must make efforts to implement activities which raise service levels – in effect; they must accept that how people feel is important to success. Where there are functions that interact with customers, it is critical for strategies to be in place to promote acceptance of this within the organization. Often the service organizations are left to do this on their own when it should be reflected in the overall ethos and delivery by the entire organization. Anything less will lead to imbalance in service delivery and constant remedial activities, which are more costly.

The prescriptions from each scenario are captured below to provide a collective view of opportunities that organizations could capitalize on. They may already have been implemented in some ways but hopefully this serves as a reminder of how important they are and the value that may be derived from reinforcing them in the organization.

- **Explain the organizational principles to all employees**

- **Outline the impact of everyone's goal to organizational success**

- **Know and communicate the type of organization you want to be**

- **Create and deliver service in an environment of confidence**

- **Build on the strengths of your superstars**

- **Ensure employees earn their customer service credits**

- **Make respect a basic employment criterion**

- **Going the extra mile should be a standard offering**

- **Ensure that the customer's need is known**

- **Make customers king of the operation**

- **Caring is part of the service offering**

- **Promote the power of positive impressions**

- **Don't take the customers right to choose for granted**

- **Service delivery is a value chain everyone should understand**

- **Make all communication respectful**

- **Proactive resolutions create a winning opportunity**

- **Delivering quality service comes from all levels**

- **Plan to exceed customer expectations**

- **Never stop reinforcing the basics**

- **The customer's expectations are always rising**

My hope is that in reading these chapters, there would be an acceptance of the base principles followed by appropriate action to invest more in the quality of service delivery. The prescriptions are not being proposed as wholesale changes but as enhancements to models that currently exist. The key is to accept that the service delivery model must have as a key outcome the creation of positive feelings within customers.

There is always the possibility of a sceptical reaction to what is being proposed. Some may think they have heard, and done, it all with regards to delivering service to customers. What I have concluded as I put this all together was that each day was a new chapter in the experiences of each customer. With this realization, both as a customer and a service delivery professional, I am even more aware that the factor of peoples' feelings must be part of the models of success developed for an organization. Irrespective of size and scope, each business must, at a minimum, acknowledge the feelings of the customer.

I read a book titled *"The No Asshole Rule"* by Dr. Robert Sutton, which outlined behaviours which limit the capacity of an organization. While he acknowledged that there may be a majority of "good" people in many organizations, his message was that the "bad" people could have an impact if not controlled. I would like to promote through the prescriptions outlined in this book, the potential of those who acknowledge the power of good. Organizations can be transformed over time, in many different ways, by those emanating this power of good. If the majority embrace the culture that places people in their rightful place on the food chain, a successful organization which constantly meets customers' needs will develop. If a premium is placed on how people feel, both inside and outside the company, an enviable model will be the outcome plus the bonus of satisfied customers.

Endnotes

1. This quote was taken from *In Search of Excellence* by Thomas Peters. This was the start for chapter 6, "Close to the Customer".

2. Article by Brian O'Keefe in *Fortune* for September 27, 2010.